D1273104

MUTUAL SURVIVAL

The Goal of
Unions and Management

MUTUAL SURVIVAL

The Goal of Unions and Management

BY

E. WIGHT BAKKE

Sterling Professor of Economics
and Industrial Administration
Yale University

SECOND EDITION

ARCHON BOOKS
Hamden, Connecticut
1966

Library Of Congress Catalog Card Number: 66-18646
Printed In The United States Of America

CONTENTS

FOREWORD

THIS book contains two appraisals of the state of union management relations in the United States. The first was made in 1946, right after World War II. The second was made twenty years later in 1966.

Part One, "The Desire for Sovereignty" is based on research undertaken at the Yale Labor and Management Center. For three years the research staff of the Center had been conducting studies of bargaining relationships between a number of specific companies and unions. From those studies had come certain hunches as to the essential character and dynamics of union organization, and of the world of management and of workers into which the union comes, and concerning the adjustments which had proved effective in making these consistent with each other. In order to test these hunches the author visited nine major centers of industrial activity in the East and Middle West and interviewed sixty each of leading representatives of management and organized labor in these centers. These representatives had been recommended as persons of broad interest and experience with collective bargaining and who were thoughtful about that experience. The attempt was made to tap all shades of reaction from that which was exceptionally antagonistic to that which was unusually cooperative.

Each of these men was encouraged to speak freely, under a pledge of strict confidence, concerning his relations with management or organized labor, as the case might be, and concerning the nature of his own task which placed compulsions upon him in his dealings with the other party.

Their comments were recorded immediately after the interview. As quoted in this book the substance of those comments remains unchanged. Editorial changes have been made in only two respects. A certain amount of profanity has been eliminated, and specific names and places have been altered or deleted in order to avoid any possible identification of the person whose words are quoted.

Their replies contributed greatly to enlarge the understanding, on the part of the staff of the Center, of the basic determinants of human behaviour in union-management relations. It was our conviction that a brief analytical summary of those replies would prove of immediate interest to a larger group concerned with making those relations more effective, productive, and satisfactory. The result was the first edition of *Mutual Survival* which constitutes Part One of the present edition.

The chapters in Part One are arranged in inverse order of their production. The first step was to record the comments made. The second was to analyze and organize these comments and point up the recurring points of emphasis. Finally the attempt was made to find in the materials the basic nature of the conflict between management and unions as they face the future. This concluding statement appears as the first chapter. It is followed by the materials upon which it is based.

The basic problem which stood out in that 1946 appraisal of the state of industrial relations was the impact of the desire for sovereignty on the part of both management and unions and of the attempts of each party to realize that desired result in the face of the efforts of the other party to do the same thing. Hence the title given to Part One. That problem is still very much alive twenty years later.

Part Two is based on the cumulative experience of the author both as an analyst of the events since 1946 in the field of industrial relations and as a practitioner involved in the continuing attempts of the parties to work out satisfactorily their relations with each other. Part Two is, therefore, a report, not so much on research activity, as on the observation of and participation in the parade of events created by the problem solvers among managerial and union leaders. The first opportunity to do this came in the writing of my presidential address for the Industrial Relations Research Association in 1958, twelve years after the first edition of *Mutual Survival.* Now eight years later, I have adapted that address to take account of what has transpired since 1958.

Both management and unions have survived that 20 years of

trial and error by building a system of collective bargaining which, while recognizing the existence of conflicts of interest between them, provides a problem solving mechanism which enables the parties to live together tolerably well. If their relationship cannot always be described as "peaceful coexistence" it is at least a "working coexistence" which probably serves the interests both of the parties and the public better than the alternative relationships of outright class warfare or submission of workers to unilateral management decisions. I have labeled my conception of that present relationship as "antagonistic cooperation." Hence the title of Part Two.

E. WIGHT BAKKE

New Haven
April 2, 1966.

MUTUAL SURVIVAL

PART ONE

The Desire for Sovereignty, 1946

I

EFFECTIVE UNIONS AND SOUND MANAGEMENT

DURING the last ten years millions of workers joined unions for the first time, thousands of them were elected to offices for which they had little training, and thousands of employers had to readjust their operations to make a place for unions. Even employers and labor leaders who were old hands at collective bargaining had never operated on such a broad front. Making collective bargaining work was a task of staggering proportions. It was not only that people had to learn how to negotiate. The difficulty went deeper than that. The negotiators didn't really understand why the other party was compelled to act as he did. Labor leaders didn't always understand the job of management, and management didn't always understand the job of labor leaders. Even when they did, the people down the line in the organization had little conception of the practical problems, the responsibilities, the traditional codes and practices, the convictions which had been developed by each group in the school of hard knocks in which they had taken their training.

Both knew that they had to learn to live and work together. They realized that the industrial warfare which preceded widespread collective bargaining had left a lot of bitterness and distrust on both sides. But they hoped that such feelings would be reduced when they got better acquainted and went to work on common problems. The difficulties that have arisen, however, are making many of them wonder whether they were not over-optimistic. The problems seem to be on the increase, not on the wane.

Last fall I went to nine major industrial centers and interviewed about sixty leaders in management and sixty leaders in the unions. I asked each of them what their chief difficulties were in dealing with the other. I tried to see through their answers and learn how each thought of his job. What were management's convictions about workable industrial relations? What were the union leaders' convictions about the basic nature of unionism? Why were these convictions what they were? How were they rooted in the job each had to do in order to survive?

I could not avoid a major conclusion. At the basis of most specific difficulties reported was the fact that both management and union leaders were expecting the other to behave in a way which each believed was impossible if they were to survive. Each was expecting peace on terms consistent with his own sovereignty. Let me be more specific. Management anticipated peace when the unions became the kind of organizations which fitted in with management's conception of the principles of workable industrial relations. Union leaders expected peace when management accepted and bargained in good faith with unions as they were in their essential characteristics. Both were willing that their tactics and strategies should change, but not the principles of sound management on the one hand or the principles of effective unionism on the other. That was a natural reaction because those principles on both sides had grown out of experience. They were the end products of trial and error. Men knew their jobs, their responsibilities, and the rewards they could expect if they operated that way. It was a stubborn reaction because men identified the survival of their organizations with the maintenance of those principles.

The plain fact is that management's convictions about sound management and the union leaders' convictions about effective unionism don't fit together at important points. Someone is going to have to modify his convictions enough to make workable mutual relations possible unless we want to face a struggle for dominance. It is not my purpose to suggest whether one or the other or both must give way. My simple objective is to lay those two sets of convictions side by side, to demonstrate the basic nature of the conflict between them, and to indicate the prospects for the reduction of that conflict.

Management Guideposts

What is management's idea of workable industrial relations? Briefly summarized, the points that stand out, almost without exception, in management's discussion of its problems are these:

Industrial relations are primarily and basically a matter of relations between management and employees, its own employees.
The first objective of industrial relations, like that of every function of management, is the economic welfare of the particular company.
Industrial relations arrangements must leave unimpaired management's prerogatives and freedom essential to the meeting of management's responsibilities.
All parties to industrial relations should be business-like and responsible.

These are the guideposts by which management determines whether it is on the road of sound industrial relations. They believe that if the unions will stay on that road, collective bargaining can be made to work. Now if the convictions of labor leaders about the essential nature of unionism turned out to be an accurate reflection of what unions have to be in order to survive, could they follow that road? That is the question I want to raise.

Labor Is "Our Men"

Look at management guidepost number one: Industrial relations are relations between a particular management and its own employees. Labor is "our men", not workers in general, not members of the union, not "organized labor." The union has a legitimate function on the basis of this principle only as the representative of, or spokesman for, "our men" and as a medium of communication with them.

Two features of unionism are incompatible with this management position. The first is that the union normally represents members in many companies throughout the industry or occupation. Every expansion of the union into new territory increases its task of representing, and maintaining group solidarity among, all workers in its jurisdiction. More and more, unions will be guided by that fact and not merely by their responsibility as spokesmen for the employees of a particular company.

In the process of doing this the second characteristic of unions becomes clear. They develop an institutional life of their own beyond the lives of individual members. A basic objective of that development is strength and power and prestige of the union as such. Internal conflicts must be ironed out. The membership must be bound together by a common philosophy and achievement.

Power of many sorts has to be acquired. Protection against competing unions must be sought. A strong internal government and leadership must be developed. Faced with such problems, the union officers cannot come to the bargaining table merely as spokesmen for the employees of a single company. Every demand, every counter-proposal, every compromise, must be measured against the need for survival and growth of the union itself. Even the degree to which the clearly expressed wishes of the employees themselves can be followed by union leadership must face that test.

Unions will never fit completely into this first principle of management's conception of industrial relations. With unions in the picture, the issues in industrial relations will never be reducible solely to matters affecting the welfare of "our men." Management would abdicate from a major role if it did not continuously insist on referring adjustments to that standard. Moreover, the unions cannot afford to forget their own primary interest in representing the interests of employees of particular firms; for the satisfaction of those interests is the foundation upon which their reputation for service must be built. But union leaders are convinced that even service to local groups is not a product merely of presenting persuasively to local management the expressed wishes of local groups. It is a product of the ability to back their arguments with a power broadly and firmly rooted in a supporting membership throughout the industry or occupation, and in the organizational strength of the union itself.

Objective: A Profitable and Efficient Enterprise

The second management guidepost points to the objective of industrial relations. The objective, like that of every function of management, is the profitable operation of the particular company. The management of industrial relations, no less than the management of financing, production, or marketing must add up to an efficient and profitable enterprise.

Any manager, whatever his philosophy or degree of benevolence, will "get tough" when the productiveness and profitability of his own firm starts going down. The job for which he is immediately rewarded or punished is promoting the welfare, not of the world, not of the national economy, not of the industry, but of his own company. This does not mean that he is unconcerned about these larger matters. It simply means, since industrial relations are one of the several problems of the enterprise for which he is responsible, that his dominant interest is in their impact upon his own enterprise.

Now a union in representing a broad membership and in maintaining its own existence necessarily raises issues which extend far beyond the particular problems of the particular company. The welfare of the entire membership and the strength of the union as such are seldom dependent solely upon what happens to any particular firm.

When the union demands a guarantee of exclusive or even continuing membership, or the check-off, in order to strengthen itself, many employers have said, "If you can sell yourself to our men, you can become strong. But that is your problem, not ours."

The union frequently argues wage possibilities in terms of rates of other firms and industries and localities whose internal problems are considerably different from those of the particular company involved. Sometimes they demand industry-wide terms. They raise the issues of aggregate purchasing power, full employment, human rights, the American standard of living. The management which is preoccupied with the internal problems and structure of its own company is likely to say, "What does that have to do with my problem?"

The conflict between management's idea that industrial relations are primarily a part of the operations of an individual company, and the tendency on the part of unions to introduce considerations which are beyond the effective control of a particular management, is not an insurmountable barrier to effective collective bargaining. Unions can expect few improvements in the material welfare for the employees of inefficient or unprofitable firms. Water isn't pumped from a dry well. Moreover, prominent management leaders are constantly urging employers to expand their interest in and concern for many of the problems which the union injects into the bargaining. To the extent that the economy and society become more complex, the welfare of the whole and that of the individual firm are bound more closely together.

Misunderstanding between the leaders of labor and management can, however, be reduced if labor leaders are aware of the fact that management has to put the effectiveness of its own operations first, and in some cases to reject as irrelevant the union's standards of comparison and its own needs for survival; and if leaders of management recognize the compulsion upon unions to chart their course by reference to such considerations. For while they may appear irrelevant from the point of view of a particular management, they are often exceedingly relevant from the point of view of the strength and power of the union and the interests of the workers whom the union represents.

Management Freedom

The principle written on the third management guidepost is carved deeply. It is this. Arrangements in the field of industrial relations must leave unimpaired management's prerogatives and freedoms essential to the meeting of management's responsibilities.

It is natural, and indeed necessary, for management to make this point clear. It is their claim of the right to survive. "Freedom", says management, "must be equal to responsibility." That is particularly understandable in view of the traditional freedom possessed by management to follow its own inclinations and wisdom with respect to obtaining, organizing, and directing a working force. As long as management practice and policy made it possible within the law to obtain and hold a working force with which it could produce and market a profitable product, little restriction was placed upon managerial discretion. Law, the decisions of customers, and pressure from fellow managers were the chief external restrictions. Collective bargaining, however, introduced a host of additional impediments to free action. Almost all functions of management, even those which are not concerned with the direction of workers, have become the subject of trade agreements or have been affected in important ways by such agreements.

A large part of management irritation with this development arises from specific restrictions on such items as discipline, hiring, transfers, work assignments, promotions and demotions, layoffs, the establishment and administration of work schedules and production quotas, organizational and technological innovations, the setting up and administration of wage systems, and like matters. Particularly irritating to many managements is the denial of their freedom to reward or punish individual workers in accordance with management's estimate of their individual merit and promise. Even in cases in which satisfactory working agreements have been made on such issues, management is disturbed by delays and restrictions upon quick decisions considered essential in the operations of the company. Beyond the specific restrictions involved, however, is the anxiety felt by many managers about the future; uncertainty as to where this process will end; a fear that it will eventually culminate in such stringent impairment of management's freedom that it will not be able to do its job satisfactorily.

Union Regulation

I have found no indication among labor leaders that they want to run the business or that they have a conscious plan to share with management the control of all features of the enterprise. But there are two features of unionism which promote tendencies which might seem to move step by step in this direction.

A union is an employer-regulating device. It seeks to regulate the discretion of employers, as one union leader said, "at every point where his action affects the welfare of the men." Now those points cover a broad area. In one sense there is not a single managerial function which does not fall within that area. Where will the process stop? Where can it stop if the union is to fulfill its basic objective of regulating collectively all those industrial policies and practices which affect the welfare of the men? Certainly, union leaders have no clear cut definition of the boundaries of this area. I doubt, on the basis of responses from management to my questions, whether any representative group of managers could agree upon precise boundaries.

The second feature of unionism which inevitably restricts managerial freedom is this. The union is a device to reduce or eliminate competition among workers by establishing uniform rules and standards and compelling individual workers to conform to them.

Putting it differently, the union purpose and policy is to eliminate individual bargaining. Union leaders believe this is an essential principle of unionism and collective bargaining. Unless a union can persuade or compel men to say, "On these terms and no others will we accept employment", it has left the door open to just that competition among workers which it was set up to eliminate. The bargaining power of the group as a whole is destroyed. The essence of union strength is a solid front on the conditions and terms of employment.

Freedom and Regulation

How far will this limitation of management freedom go? Is it an inevitable trend which will not be brought to a halt, short of placing management in a strait-jacket bound by which it cannot discharge its responsibilities, let alone make progress? It is hard for many employers to be optimistic about the outlook. Let me summarize several suggestions made by a number of labor and management leaders who have devised workable arrangements in this matter.

The end of this conflict between management freedom and union regulation is not in sight. But one thing is clear. Management and union leaders who have made some progress toward a solution haven't done so by arguing in terms of management "prerogatives", union "rights" and workers "interests." They worked on a less abstract level. They dealt with specific and practical definitions of the points at which management had to retain absolute control and the points at which it could share control. They focused their attention on the practical job to be done. Was joint operation or a division of labor the best way to do it? And they were each willing to resolve any conflict by an arrangement which would meet the practical, if not the abstract, needs of the other.

The leaders of the labor movement in America, with the exception of communists, are not guided by a definite philosophy on this point. They are opportunistic and pragmatic in their policy and practice. How far they go is guided by practical needs, not by any revolutionary philosophy.

One labor leader put into words an impression I got from many others. He told me that he could see this increasing restriction on management operations in almost any series of annually negotiated local contracts. Whenever he saw an added restriction, however, he said to himself, "Oh, oh, the boys had trouble or sensed trouble on that point last year." He went on, "You see, after the basic terms of employment are brought under collective control and mutual confidence is established, control at other points usually is a response to some actual or anticipated abuse of managerial discretion. If they use it to undermine the union, or pit man against man, or if the men get het up about some way they operate, why then we have to climb in and put on the screws at that point. We don't want to run the business. We want to remain free to kick and to put pressure on management."

Employers who think they see light on this problem tell me this: if they give continuous attention to the impact of their action upon the stability of the union, upon the willingness of the workers to abide by common standards, upon the satisfaction of employees with their working conditions, they will be able to judge more accurately whether any policy or practice is likely to stimulate further demands for union participation in these matters.

I am not indicating that all stimulus for such participation arises from acts of management. I am merely pointing out that the basic drive of unions is to bring an increasing area of the operations of the enterprise under the control of collective bargaining and that the drive is frequently increased by what management does.

Mutual Interests

Union leaders are acting in accordance with the basic principles of unionism in seeking to impose rules on management and to reduce competition among workers. The process itself and not its end result absorbs many of them at the moment. That is natural, particularly in the early stages of organization. But thoughtful labor leaders tell me that the time has arrived for a serious estimate of the effects of that end result upon management's ability to do its job. It is only common sense, say these leaders, if the unions expect management to be interested in the effect of its action on building effective unions, unions in turn should demonstrate an intelligent interest in the survival requirements of efficient management.

This conflict promises to be one of the most troublesome in the whole field of labor and management relations. It is particularly so because fundamental principles and survival needs are involved on both sides. Industrial peace and workable collective bargaining will depend greatly upon whether both parties can reconcile their principles on this score. Can they look upon their convictions not as absolute and eternal but as modifiable in the interests of workable arrangements, permitting each to survive and get on with his work? Management and labor leaders alike will have to test their actions by this question, "If I do this or insist on this arrangement, will it be possible for the other fellow to do his job well?" How well each can do his own job depends on how well the other fellow can do his.

Business-like Responsibility

The final point in management's conviction about the essentials of industrial relations is that all parties should be business-like and responsible. Much of what management says about union responsibility is another way of expressing their conviction that unions, in their dealings with management, should be business-like. This, they insist, is a reasonable expectancy. But its realization is not as simple as it sounds. I think it is well to recognize that management's definition of "business-like" and "responsibility" grows out of its own experience in doing business; that what is meant is "following the rules of business." This is no place for an extended dissertation on these rules but certain of the more important of them should be recalled. What are they?

First of all, parties to a business arrangement should be free to accept or reject any offer or proposal on the basis of their interpretation of the benefit of such action to them. There should be no compulsion upon them to do otherwise. There is no place, at least in the theory of free business competition, for duress exerted by one party upon another. In the second place, all affairs should be conducted upon the basis of reasonable and orderly procedures which are understood and accepted by both parties. In the third place, the bargains made through these processes should be reducible to definite contracts equally binding upon both parties. In the fourth place, those who make the contracts should have the ability to deliver and to hold any parties for whom they are agents to the arrangements made. In the fifth place, if they are not able to deliver, redress should be available through agreed upon penalties voluntarily accepted and, if not, enforced by the courts.

Source of Business Code

Where did these rules come from? Their source is in business experience. They are the rules which embody the wisdom of that experience in dealings between business men. What I would like to suggest is that the business man's definition of business-like conduct and responsible conduct is that which he has found satisfactory in governing the relations between manufacturing concerns, banks, insurance companies, dealers, brokers, and the like. People who manage such institutions are motivated and guided by primarily business considerations, those of economic gain or loss. Their code of conduct is a response to that fact, although it may also be an excellent code of conduct from a moral and from a practical point of view.

Moreover, because business is so important a part of our common life, such rules are pretty generally applied to all human relations. In a business civilization the code of business dealing tends to be imposed on every one. I am not suggesting that it should be otherwise, particularly when people are making business deals. Persons who are not primarily business men, however, and institutions which are not solely business organizations, have non-business problems. Sometimes what they have to do can't be done by following the rules of business. They develop a code of their own which doesn't always jibe with the business man's code. If the business man has to do business with such people or institutions, he is naturally exasperated. But a practical solution is more nearly possible if he understands why the other behaves as he does.

Are Unions Business Concerns?

Now, suppose a union turned out to be not primarily or exclusively a business concern—what then? Would its leaders feel as thoroughly committed to the rules of business?

Let me say immediately that there is a large element in the function of the union which is definable as business operations. A union is in part a business institution, but it has other features which keep it from being purely a business organization. Let me cite a few of these characteristics which are prominent in union leaders' conceptions of unionism, and which, when added together, raise a serious question as to whether unions will ever be guided solely by the code of business operations.

A union is a part of a working class *movement.* A movement is not a business. To the degree that workers are thoroughly integrated with it, they are bound by psychological ties of loyalty, not only to a particular union but to the movement with its traditions, folklore, and symbols. There is nothing in the world of business which compares exactly to the song books, the banners, the pilgrimages, the traditions of struggle against exploitation, the folklore of martyrdom, the poetry and literature which mirror in their various phases the psychological sentiments which hold a movement together and motivate much of the conduct of participants. A movement is not a business, although it may have business functions to perform. Loyalty to this movement on the part of a significant nucleus of union men will very frequently cause them to set aside purely business considerations and to adopt tactics which are anything but business-like.

Again, a union is a pressure organization originating in the desire on the part of a group of people with relatively little power to influence the action of a group with relatively more power. The words "struggle" and "fight" and "battle" and "crusade" are not merely a part of the vocabulary of union organizers. They are symbols of the conception which these men hold of their own task, symbols made vivid by their life experience. The tactics and policies of today are molded by the experiences of yesterday.

Furthermore a union is a device for continuously changing the balance of fundamental economic rights and rewards in favor of workers. A business is a device for obtaining economic advantages within the framework of established rights. But it is one of the major functions of unions to alter the balance of these rights and rewards as between employers and workers. The changing of fundamental rights, at best, is more of a political than a business procedure. In many cases, its tactics point more in the direction of warfare than in the direction of trade.

Finally a union is a political institution in its internal structure and procedures. The solidarity of its participants is affected, not by the business-like procedures of hiring and firing, the giving and withholding of economic rewards, but by the techniques well known to political leaders. A moment's reflection upon the methods of political machines and the conditions of their survival will amply demonstrate the difficulties in the way of unions ever becoming pure business organizations. Or consider an analogy from business itself. Suppose management had to get the consent of stockholders to practically every decision made. Suppose that their operations involved the constant and detailed activity of stockholders. Suppose that a stockholder, dissatisfied by this day to day activity, could object, not by selling his stock to someone else but by actually withdrawing capital from the business. Management would then be compelled to develop in relation to their stockholders the same kind of political strategies which union leaders must develop in relation to their members. The ability on the part of management to make binding decisions which they have the power to carry through in their dealings with others would be immensely complicated if they had to depend on detailed support and cooperation from stockholders in order to implement their decisions. Management-stockholder relations would become political, not solely business relations.

If it is understood that unions are, internally, political organizations, then much that is referred to as unbusiness-like or irresponsible conduct may be set down as the behaviour of a political institution which has not yet solidified and regularized its own structure or become adapted to the task at hand. I can imagine, for instance, that if a large city were to be run by the methods of town meeting democracy, the confusion and ineptness and inadequacy of the actions taken might conceivably be labelled as irresponsible by those accustomed to a city-manager form of government. There is no *democratic* short cut to the development of well integrated and disciplined political institutions.

Basis of Workable Arrangements

These features of unionism retard, if they do not make impossible, the development of unions completely responsive to the principle of business-like dealings and responsibility so important in management's conception of industrial relations. They are not cited in order to demonstrate an ultimate incompatibility between unions and this conception, but to indicate the character of the problem faced.

It is a difficult problem, but I have met men in unions and in management who think it is not insurmountable. They are living with it and making some progress. What are the points on which they are agreed; how have they approached the problem?

Collective Bargaining a Business Process

They agree that, whatever the nature and backgrounds of management and unions, collective bargaining is largely a business process, particularly after the union is genuinely accepted as a participant in the enterprise. Hence it is not unreasonable to expect both parties to be business-like and to act responsibly in observing business contracts. If the contract proves unsatisfactory to either party, the thing to do is to correct the situation when a new contract is made, not to "chisel" on or tear up the present one. That attitude is basic.

Codes Develop Slowly

The second point is equally important. It takes time for men and institutions to adapt their code of behaviour to the realities of their relationships. The code of business dealings was not produced in a day. And it was not immediately embraced by all business men. Even today the observance isn't 100%. Historically, business enterprise, itself, replaced forms of the struggle for self-maintenance which were more war-like and predatory. Many generations were to pass before the modern code of business was produced and won general acceptance. Business men have at least a hundred years' start on union leaders in the traditions of contract making and contract keeping.

Acceptable Codes Are Rewarding

In the third place they approach the problem realizing that men tend to accept that code which rewards them. Business men accept this code because in the kind of a world we live in they are rewarded in the achievement of their basic objectives by observing it. If the unions accept it, it will be for the same reason. It is possible that the objectives of some unions are such that they cannot be reached by the utilization of purely business methods, which is another way of saying that business-like methods and codes alone may not be able to reward them. But as the major features of exploitation and inequalities are reduced in importance on the American industrial scene, as the memories of past struggles become less vivid, and as unions are accepted as legitimate participants in business enterprise, it should not be beyond the realm of reasonable hope to anticipate that responsible, business-like action would prove more rewarding to unions than its opposite.

Unions have to deal with business men. Much of their activity is a business operation. The business code is a hard fact to which they must adapt themselves. But any code which is mutually acceptable has to be mutually workable, that is, it has to be mutually advantageous and rewarding.

Codes Change

Another point of agreement between men who appear to be making some progress on this matter is the recognition that the code itself is not an eternal law. It is still changing. Since it has to be satisfactory to both parties to the relationship which it governs, the interests, the problems, the necessary behaviour of any new party have to be considered. When they are, the code undergoes change, possibly for the better. It is no criticism of the business code to say that it grew up to govern relations between men who were producing or exchanging property and commodities with economic gain in mind. Even the labor contract was supposed to be one for a sale of and payment for a commodity, namely labor skill. The worker was a business man marketing what he had to sell. Well, he was marketing himself, a human being, not a bar of steel or a package of corn flakes. Unions are not solely responsible for putting that idea across, but their influence in changing the code on the point can't be ignored.

Unions have also had their own codes modified by experience in business dealings. Said one labor leader, "I was trained as a fighter for human rights. I'm not forgetting that. But there's more ways than one to fight. It comes down to a question of method. If you can win your point by negotiation and making better contracts every year, why trot out the artillery? But there's rules to follow if the method of negotiations and contracts is to work. The employers I deal with have had a lot of experience in developing rules that fit that method. I've profited by their experience. The rules don't always fit the human relations involved, though. But if I want the method to work, it's my job to make the rules fit, not to throw them completely out the window and grab the employer by the throat."

The point is that the code of business is an evolving code. It can be made a better one if it fits the realistic nature of the human relations which it governs. Collective bargaining has provided for some employers and labor leaders the chance to get acquainted with those realities and to make the code better and more workable.

Organizational Responsibility

Another point made by these men who think they are making progress is this: the observance of contracts, much more than their negotiation, depends, not so much on the character of officers as upon the organizations they lead. The charges fly from both sides, "The fellow at the top means well, but the men down the line have different ideas. Then what happens to the contract you've made?"

Those charges underscore the point. Both management and unions can be really responsible only to the extent that the whole organization is back of and acts in line with the decisions of its leaders. Both have a job to do on this score. Management has some advantage in the fact that its structure of organization is better established and that "the fellow at the top" can replace the "men down the line" if they resist persuasion. Union leaders have greater difficulty in firing those who upset the apple cart. The organizational structure of a political institution like a union is more easily upset than that of a business, unless the union officers want to throw democracy overboard. Such points reveal the problem of but do not excuse the lack of organizational discipline. One of the biggest problems on the minds of the union leaders I have met is the development of internal political structure, techniques, codes, and discipline. By this they mean techniques for exploring the needs and wants of members, the establishment of recognized patterns of leadership and authority, the development of a disciplined citizenship within the union committed to action in accordance with the decisions of their representatives.

The final point made by these men is that in this period of learning to live and work together, a good many rough spots can be made smooth, inevitably inadequate machinery can function better, and conflicting codes cause less damage to good relations, if labor leaders and management can associate and get to know each other in other ways than as bargainers or grievance settlers.

The Issue: Mutual Survival

In conclusion I would like to make two points clear. I have made no judgment about what is right and what is wrong, either in management's convictions about the essentials of industrial relations or in the convictions held by union leaders about the essentials of unionism. I don't know what is right or wrong. But I am sure of one thing, nothing is right which won't work; and arrangements that work are going to have to be reconciled with these convictions and survival needs on both sides. Unless methods are adapted to such realities, we shall presently find ourselves repeating the words of the March Hare in *Alice in Wonderland.* You recall he had tried to fix the Mad Hatter's watch with butter. When his method did not work, he could only express his bewilderment in these words, "And it was the *best* butter too, the *best* butter."

In the second place I have offered no solution for reconciling those convictions. That solution will have to be hammered out by practical men in the light of the whole set of problems they face. I don't know all those problems. I have never met a payroll for more than 16 people and I have never organized a union. Every suggestion I have made has been relayed from practical men of experience on whose shoulders rests the responsibility for practical action.

Both management and labor leaders will be better equipped for such practical action, however, if they know thoroughly the kind of a job and responsibilities faced by the other, and his convictions about what is required if he and his organization are to survive. Men will fight when they believe their survival is threatened. The first task of life is to live. I am convinced that the great majority of employers and labor leaders alike are not out to "bust" or "hamstring" or take over the other. But they can do that without intending to do so by fighting for their own survival in ways which endanger the survival of the other. The end result will be the overwhelming of both free management and free unions. The chain of events is too clear to miss. If either union leaders or management expect, or try to force, the other to be what they honestly believe they cannot be and survive, they will arouse the fighting opposition of the other, bring out the very belligerent and stubborn characteristics which make peace impossible. If two such giants as organized labor and organized management engage in a struggle for dominance within the highly delicate mechanism of the American economy, neither can win and Democracy is bound to lose. They will all go down together in the resulting chaos or in the regimentation which will arise from public demand to avoid chaos. Free unions, free management, free enterprise, and a free society will survive or go under together.

Mutual survival, not separate survival! That is our common aim. If we keep it steadily before us we can avoid a fanatical struggle for dominance which can never be won within a Democracy.

II

MANAGEMENT LOOKS AT THE UNIONS

THE chapters which follow contain the materials from which were derived the conclusions set forth in the preceding chapter.

Management in American industry is not unanimous in its expression of hopes or anxieties with respect to collective bargaining. Nor can management reaction to dealing with unions be defined as uniformly favorable or unfavorable. This much can be said: all have experienced difficulties in their attempts to integrate collective bargaining into their practice and ideas. Many are optimistic with respect to the possibility of removing these difficulties. Many are troubled. Some are bewildered. Others are resentful and angry. But most are convinced that unions are here to stay and that management must discover or develop the means of living with them and carrying on their tasks as managers in collaboration with organizations of their employees.

All managers interviewed indicate difficulties in the seven areas listed below as they wrestled with this problem of collaboration. No one, of course, cited from his own experience all of the examples given to illustrate the nature of these difficulties.

The following analytical summary of responses to my question, "What attitudes, practices and policies of unions provide you with your greatest problems in the conduct of your industrial relations and in operating your business?" carries with it no conclusion or moral judgment on my part. It is a true report of the reactions of over sixty employers in major industrial centers of the country. It is presented in the conviction that the achievement of industrial peace must be built upon a full and frank recognition of the actual reactions of men to their problems, and upon a realization of *their* convictions as to the nature of these problems.

The statement of the problem in each case is amplified in three ways. First, examples are given of the sort of experiences with union practices the major characteristic of which is represented by the statement. Second, are listed the underlying assumptions which management feels are held by union leaders in carrying on such practices. Third, under the heading of "Favorable Factors" are recorded some of the experiences of management which suggest that the difficulty named is not insurmountable, that there are compensating values in collective bargaining.

The summary of management's major problems in dealing with unions follows.

Infringement on Management Functions, Prerogatives and Freedom

Examples

Reduction of management's freedom to make *quick* decisions when such are required in order to get a competitive advantage or clear up a production difficulty. Such decisions often affect matters which by agreement are subject to negotiation with the union.

Interference with management's organization and direction of the working force, particularly in hiring (closed shop), transfers, work assignments, promotions and demotions, layoffs, especially by means of seniority rules.

Interference in disciplinary action.

Restrictions on establishment and administration of work schedules and production quotas considered essential to effective and economic operation of the plant.

Resistance to, or attempts to control, managerial and technological innovations.

Demand for direct or indirect determination of the wage system and for control over its standards and functioning.

Insertion into wage negotiations of company policy on prices, volume, and profit distribution.

Indications that the infringement has no definable limits.

Assumptions

All areas of decision affecting workers' status in, relation to, and conditions of employment should be subject to negotiation and covered by jointly determined rules.

These areas are practically unlimited and are enlarging.

Favorable Factors

Definite values have been realized from union participation.

Management has been made acutely aware that implementation of decisions through junior management actually affects the nature of a decision.

The union has in many cases provided an efficient medium for carrying out managerial functions:
- Provision of means of learning of trouble spots before they get too big to handle or fester because of lack of attention.
- Provision of a "no" element for preventing practices and policies which junior management might agree to against better judgment in deference to top management.
- Provision of possibility for organized cooperation in the task of production when mutual confidence can be established. Realization of untapped sources of improvement in the production process.
- Preventative of high-handed management.

The causation of infringement does not appear to lie in any deep-seated union objective or policy with respect to taking over management.
- The experience of actual infringement is bound to be vivid at the moment for two reasons:
  - Industry is moving from an era of nearly complete managerial discretion to one of joint participation. Every move reduces discretion at some point.
  - The process is still colored by the atmosphere of conflict and struggle for power; it is not natural that the aggressor should say, "This far and no farther."
- Once basic security of the union is assured and major areas are brought under collective control, the infringement appears to be motivated by two considerations:
  - Is control over this area necessary to guard against undermining of union solidarity?
  - Is control over this area necessary in order to meet dissatisfaction of workers with management's use of discretionary powers during the past year?
- Management can forestall such demands by wise industrial relations.

Reduction of Possibility of Individual Adjustments and Imposition of Common Standards and Rules

Examples

Quota setting and restrictions on individual production.

Refusal to permit large variations in production and compensation in proportion to energy, skill, and ambitions of workers.

Insistence on bringing the best to the level of the average worker.

Restrictions on making awards in promotion and transfer to other jobs on basis of merit.

Automatic progression schedules.

Denial of access of the individual worker to management directly by insistence that union representative be present in first step of grievance procedure.

Assumptions

The interest of the group is paramount. The individual must conform.

All terms of employment should be uniform and not subject to the competitive action of individuals.

Favorable Factors

Most adjustments have to be group-wide anyway to avoid evidence of unfairness and injustice; dealing with the union on general rules provides evidence of good faith and nondiscriminatory exercise of management functions.

When large numbers are involved, orderly and clearly understood procedures are required. Dealing with the union provides rules and definitions which make group-wide adjustments more orderly.

Since union negotiations normally end in a formal and definite representation of policy, rules, and definitions, the progressive amendment of this policy becomes more logical and orderly.

A particular hothead's ideas tend to become integrated with a general policy. There is some reduction of anarchy in industrial relations.

Management implies organization, and collective bargaining is one way of organizing relations with employees in a way which gives consideration to the basic problems which management alone would not discover.

Development of Loyalty of Workers Toward the Union by Means Which Reduce Loyalty to the Firm

Examples

Emphasis upon all exploitation, past and present, as a reason for union solidarity regardless of the attitude of the particular company.

Emphasis on exploitive features of the employer's role to the neglect of his services to workers.

Stressing need of protection from the employer.

Usurpation of management's role as leader and director of workers' welfare and relegation of employer to position of one who must be pressured into concessions.

Demanding of joint credit for action favorable to employees even when this comes spontaneously on management's initiative.

Development of antagonisms toward the employer, some fancied, some real, rather than trying to eliminate them.

Attacks upon management's good faith and integrity, particularly when facts are misrepresented.

Assumptions

There is a basic antagonism of interest between management and workers.

The union is the only one who can be trusted truly to be interested in and to promote the workers' welfare.

Any tactics are justified which increase group solidarity.

Favorable Factors

An institutional means for promoting workers' interests geared to their own way of life and in which they can fully participate has definite appeal to workers over management-managed means.

Management's conception of "company interests" is dominated by their own problems. Loyalty to "company" defined in such terms is not broad enough to win full response from workers nor a basis for real collaboration with them. The union can represent and make clear other interests.

The union provides management with an opportunity for contact with labor leaders who in turn can transmit to the workers a clearer conception of management's problems, if they will.

The union provides an avenue of education for workers on management's problems which does not bear the onus of management propaganda.

Loyalty to a genuine workers' organization is not incompatible with loyalty to the company unless the latter is undermined as a technique of obtaining union solidarity.

Loyalty is a product of participation and if the union increases a genuine sense of participation by workers in the company's affairs, that loyalty may be increased.

Entrance of a Third Party and Injection of Issues Irrelevant to Company Welfare Into the Firm's Industrial Relations

Examples

Necessity of dealing with non-employees whose attitudes and reactions are inconsistent with those management believes characterize its employees.

Dealing with outsiders who do not understand the internal structure and problems of the firm.

Dealing with those who have no legal responsibility for success of the firm and over whom management has no control.

Insistence on protective devices for the union as such; for example, closed shop and check-off.

Demands and practices rooted in needs of internal union politics and career opportunities for union leadership.

Demands rooted in jurisdictional conflicts.

Demand for industry-wide terms.

Use of other firms, often in other industries, as standards of comparison.

Origin of demands in union's objectives with respect to political power.

Assumptions

Outsiders know and can protect the interests of the men better than the men themselves.

It is necessary to have a buffer between men and management.

The strength and solidarity of the union as such is a legitimate consideration to be weighed in negotiation of terms.

The needs and problems of the particular firm are not the only or even the primary basis upon which adjustments should be sought.

Men without responsibility for ultimate success of firm have a legitimate right to participate in controlling the firm's operations.

Favorable Factors

District and national officers frequently provide more intelligent leadership than that available from local officers with respect to overall problems of the firm and industry.

An interpretive medium is provided between management and workers whose ways, experience, and functions are so different that direct understanding is difficult. At its best, the interpretation can work both ways.

A strong union has greater possibility of being a responsible union.

Injection of "outside" considerations provides a stimulus toward giving greater scope to the firm's policy and practice, and points up factors and forces which progressive management ought to consider.

A constant reminder is provided of the changing character of the factors outside of those immediately relevant to the productive process which have long-range effects on that process.

An instrument is available for reduction of unfair competition between firms in the utilization of human resources.

The very fact that unions must consider the impact of their policy and practice with respect to one firm upon the satisfaction of workers in other firms is often a fact contributing to conservatism in demands.

Use of "Unsound" Economics

Examples

Insufficient attention to or ignoring of:

- Cost problems and the relation of costs to prices, of prices to volume, and of volume to employment.
- The role of profits in economic processes.
- The importance of risk capital, expansion reserves, etc.
- Relation of man-hour productivity to possibilities in hourly wages.

Emphasis on "purchasing power" theories without consideration of their relevance to the operations of a particular firm.

Concentration of attention on money earnings.

Hours and pace of work demands intended to stretch out the job.
Lack of interest in the tax burden imposed by social benefits legislation.
No matter how much is granted at one time, the next time *more* will be asked.

Assumptions

The economic problems of individual employers are similar to those of the economy as a whole.
Wages come out of a fund which employer is trying to reduce as little as possible.
The employer is trying to buy labor as cheaply as possible.
The essential problem is the employer's selfish attitude.
More money in the pocket means a higher standard of living.
More even distribution of income is a good thing in itself.
Wider economic effects will be beneficial if each group gets as much as possible for itself.
"Lump of labor" theory.
Every contract should represent a gain, not only absolutely, but in the relative share of proceeds of enterprise going to workers.

Favorable Factors

A stimulus is given employers to broaden their concept of economic realities and to integrate management's economic interests with those of the larger economy.
A stimulus is offered to management to consider the economic advantages in maintaining and improving the human resources which they employ.
Continuous upping of demands is a constant incentive to finding other ways of reducing costs.
The union position is a revelation of issues which management must meet in order to educate workers as to the mutual economic interest of management and workers.
Some unions are developing a systematic and penetrating research into the economics of industry which can teach that management whose economic horizon is limited.

Irresponsible and Insincere Conduct Toward Employer

Examples

Bargaining backed by threat of coercion and actual hair-trigger willingness to use force as a matter of policy.
Use of force in the form of the strike or slowdown before contract procedure is exhausted or before negotiations are given a chance, especially in violation of an agreement.
Strikes without notice and without a statement of demands.
Strikes against the decision of a non-company agency.
Strikes for recognition or for organizing purposes.

Sympathy strikes.
Restriction of output and make-work.
Attempts to make "special deals" outside of contract whenever that agreement pinches some internal union interest.
"Making" grievances and dissatisfactions or amplifying them unreasonably.
Unfair and untrue representation to the men of employer's position and practices.
Failure of leadership to carry through on agreements made with management, and inability to "deliver" and keep the membership in line with the agreement.
Resistance to accepting contract obligations.
Lack of interest in the welfare of the company.

Assumptions

Force or coercion is an essential and legitimate device in bargaining.
The strike is labor's most essential device and most precious right to be employed not under social restrictions but as expediency dictates.
The end justifies the means.
Might makes right.
There is a basic antagonism of interest between management and workers.
Agreements are sacred only so long as they serve immediate expediency.
Contract obligations are one sided, and making contracts means imposing restrictions on employer discretion.

Favorable Factors

Some signs of development of the organization, leadership, and rules which are a prerequisite alike to effective union action and to responsible action under law.
Many objectionable present tactics are designed to develop group solidarity, which is an essential condition for group responsibility.
A stimulus is provided for management consideration of how much its own attitude and practice produces trouble with the union.
Emphasis by top union officials on the need for and methods of local responsible action is increasing.
Growth in the observable capacity for responsible action on the part of some union leaders.

Irresponsible and Undemocratic Conduct of Internal Union Affairs

Examples

Resort to coercion on individual workers to join the union and maintain group solidarity.
Lack of democratic elections and procedures for discovering membership

needs and obtaining approval for arrangements designed to meet them.
Lack of financial accounting.

Assumptions

The end of union internal activity is power and group solidarity; the type of internal procedure and organization is subsidiary to this objective.
The union's internal affairs are nobody's business. If members don't object, why should anyone else?

Favorable Factors

Employers were not familiar enough with the actual internal affairs of the unions to identify considerations which might reduce their anxieties on this score.

III

MANAGEMENT SPEAKS FOR ITSELF

THE preceding chapter outlined the major favorable and unfavorable reactions of management with respect to dealing with unions. The points were presented in this form in order that the reader might have a brief overall picture of the chief items in the thinking of management on this subject. Some of the particularly interesting comments illustrating the experience of management are presented below.

INFRINGEMENT ON MANAGEMENT FUNCTIONS, PREROGATIVES, AND FREEDOM

(1) They say, the most reasonable of them, that they want a voice in whatever affects the men. That sounds reasonable enough, and I agree with it. But that covers just about everything you do in production, because the welfare of the men is certainly involved from start to finish. I don't disagree that they shouldn't have a voice in it through their union, but there's got to come a point where the last word must be had by the man responsible, and sometimes the word has got to come quick before you have time to involve the union or it's too late.

Take discipline for instance. Granted it's sometimes abused. We have a rule, any men caught fighting, both of them are fired—at once. This is a plain safety rule in a plant of our kind, so important that we felt judgment had to be fast and sure, even if we made a mistake once in a while. But the union wants in on that. After a long argument we gave in. They're not fired now, just suspended, and if the union wants to take it up, they can, within five days. At first they challenged every one; now they are more discriminating. I'll say that for them, and I suppose some injustices are prevented. But the fact remains that the foreman has lost influence; and here's the important thing, there's more cases of fighting.

Another case, allocation to jobs. On the whole any sensible management wants to do the allocating in order to get the most efficiency, and to put the right and best men on the job. In new jobs, or in making transfers considered promotions, seniority gets in your way. On lay-offs, in order to keep the best organization and the most efficient you have to be discriminating. Order of hiring has little to do with it.

Or we develop a new product, decide to set up a new department in one of our Tennessee plants and another one in Ohio. We want to pick our men to train for that department. Natural enough. We say to the union, "Let us pick the men for six months without any bidding on basis of seniority, then, when they're a trained nucleus, we'll go back to seniority bidding." The union officers say, "Okay!" The membership turns it down. I've been working on that one a month and the upshot is that unless the national officers can bring the boys around, we just can't set up in that place. We'll lose because that's the best place for the plant. The men will lose in employment opportunities and the union will lose members. It may work out all right but we've lost a good month of production that in the old days we would have had.

(2) Restriction on management freedom is a big issue. This isn't breastbeating. We've got heavy responsibilities for making quick, accurate, and effective decisions. Sometimes there are considerations that we can't divulge or that wouldn't be understood if we did. We're held responsible for the success of them but the union isn't. It takes complicated maneuvering to run a business and all of the parts have to be kept working together. You have to have a good deal of free play in the rope for that. Sometimes there's a particular restriction that gets your goat, but on the whole it's the overall sense of being closed in on, and the anticipation of more of the same, that gets you. It's the cumulative effect of one area of freedom after another being reduced and the promise of still more that gives us real concern. But you make adjustments and go on to every particular one. It's not impossible. But you wonder how long it can go on and leave you able to meet your responsibilities.

(3) The basic problems are interference in discipline and the restriction of output. It was inevitable, in view of the essential

drive and requirements of the unions, that they should try to move in on a wide area of company practice. That is what collective bargaining means. But there are some areas so vital to management that discretion at the moment seems absolutely essential. Discipline, output standards, getting the best man into the proper job, these are exceptionally important. All should be subject to grievance procedure, but initiation should be management's prerogative.

I can see the union's point, however, in trying to control at specific points, for they can't control as stockholders and directors can if the accumulated result of these policies is bad for the company and the men. They can't get rid of us. So their alternative is to control where they can, that is at the specific point of operation.

(4) It is not so much what the demand is now, but where does it all end? We can stand the rough seas if we know where we are headed. We have dealt with one union now for thirty-five years, and thirty-five years is a long time. Every year there is something new. Where will it all end? Will management end up by being employees of the union?

We've got to come to an understanding about division of functions just as we have in management; otherwise it will be chaos. We have six hundred personnel people and we have to have rules and definitions of function but if the union doesn't recognize the necessity for this regularization of principles and policy, they think we're horsing them when we fall back on "management policy" as our basic argument.

We used to be able to take quick action but now the need for negotiations, in spite of their value, slows us up when speed is necessary.

(5) I won't say the picture is all black. We haven't found it so. Of course the union gets involved now in decisions we used to make by ourselves. The area of operations which we can carry out without the union coming into the picture is narrowing down. But you have to set off against that disadvantage some advantages we couldn't get any other way. We've learned that the real decision made by management is not the order or policy statement that comes out of the front office, but the action that is carried out down the line.

Without the union we often didn't learn how that decision was altered in practice until it was too late to avoid trouble. In many cases the union can warn us of bugs in a policy before we have to learn the hard way. It is sometimes good for management to have a "no" man down the line.

(6) I wouldn't take a cool million for our labor-management cooperation supplementary agreement. Of course it means the union, and through it the men, take part in a job those of us in management used to do ourselves. And we have to let them in on information we used to suppose had to be kept under our own hats. But if we mean what we say by cooperation, that's what is involved. The trouble is that what lots of employers mean by cooperation is "Willingness to go along with what I say without objection." Sure there are risks, but Democracy has always been and always will be risky.

(7) I have found that as soon as they get involved enough to know the size of the problem, and if they trust you, they are perfectly willing to agree on a division of labor with management left free to do the job it can do better than anyone else. They aren't hatching up a plot to take over management, at least in my experience.

Reduction of Possibility of Individual Adjustments and Imposition of Common Standards and Rules

(1) We used to be able to build up morale by rewarding individuals, but now we can't do that freely and to the same extent. That is one technique destroyed. It wouldn't be so bad if the substitute method (arrangement with the union) had the same or better result, but it destroys individual initiative.

(2) Look at this article I read on foremen the other day. The same words hold good for all workers. Let me read it that way. "*The all for one and one for all* philosophy of unionism means that workers cannot be individually responsible but must deal with the company only as a group, through a union. The union arbitrarily limits responsibilities which individual workmen can assume; it tends to hold back workers who emerge from the group by out-

standing performance or service; it keeps all workers on a basis of impersonal relationship with the company."

(3) Not only should the interest of the employees be paramount, but we must also take care to consider the interests of the employees as individuals rather than be concerned with the interests of the employees as a mass. This war is being fought for the freedom of the individual from dominance by the state.

The same consideration should guide us in considering the welfare of employees with respect to their unions. The union should serve the individual rather than have the individual serve the union. The union is a means to an end, not an end in itself. And encouragement of unions by the state must not go to the point at which the union organized to serve the individual employee is put in a position where it can dictate to the individual employee.

(4) You've got to face the fact that when a company gets to the size where the policy-making individuals can't make their decisions except through joint agreement with other management people, and when the carrying out of that policy depends on the skill and ability of a line of subordinates, anything that regularizes and makes uniform that policy leads to a clear-cut definition of common rules and procedures. That is something management would have to develop for itself anyway.

Smart management can discover at least one possibility for regularization in working out with the union the problems of common standards. The technique of individual rewards is effective only when the group is small enough so that the person who administers them can be completely aware of the worker's capacities and possibilities.

Development of Loyalty of Men Toward the Union By Means Which Reduce Loyalty to the Firm

(1) Building the union is their real job and it is irrelevant to management's job. Combativeness is necessary for this group solidarity, that's what they think. I'm not sure. True, if there is no combat, the interest in the union seems to lag. What would you do in that situation? You'd keep hell-a-poppin'. There's got to be

some other way. Why can't they see that? Well, in the first place they are still organizing. The majority are only thinking of the union as a protective device. If they don't need protecting, why have a union, they think. Second, the leaders know these tactics; sometimes it's all they know. They have been trained in them, are practiced in them. They know they work. There are alternative techniques that hold a group together—education, recreation, insurance, etc., and they are trying them out timidly. But in the meantime they are not going to risk the loss of solidarity by wholehearted abdication of trouble brewing and complete reliance on other methods. In addition, they are afraid to stick their necks out.

Now let's be fair. They're young. In the first years they used these fighting methods partly out of habit, partly out of necessity. Then came the War Labor Board and the decision not to deal with labor difficulty while the men were on strike. It was more than could be expected, but the leaders went to bat and tried to quiet the hotheads. They did a swell job and nearly lost their own jobs. Some of them did. They gave the hothead minorities just the issue they wanted. Responsible leaders were punished. Now the War Labor Board is gone and can you blame them for trying to recapture their prestige?

Union organization is the real purpose of the stewards. They are not what they are supposed to be from the point of view of the employer. Really they are a police force for the union.

(2) The union should be behind workers and not between the workers and management.

(3) It is not so much the aggravation of hearing violent and untrue things said about management. That is bad enough. But it is the basic assumption which is clear, namely that collective bargaining is a battle and the ordinary rules of peaceful, reasonable procedure, and mutual respect don't hold. We try to drive a hard bargain with our suppliers and dealers too. That's business, but they don't call us fascists, blood-suckers, etc. They expect hard bargaining. Incidentally, those tactics don't create any respect for the fellow who uses them in the mind of the management even if they do make the men value the union.

(4) What troubles me is their very reasonable, respectful, and business-like attitude when we're in negotiations and then these scurrilous attacks reported in their meetings and in their papers about the same negotiations. It isn't consistent. It indicates an instability that is easily interpreted by management as a lack of dependability. But more, it indicates a fundamental conviction that they've got to make tyrants out of us in order to get the men to stick to the union.

(5) The union wants to usurp the company's leadership in workers' welfare. Take the example of group insurance. They wanted the company plan knocked out because it was company sponsored and wanted their own substituted. Upon investigation, however, they found they could not get the same benefits. We worked it out, thanks to a national officer, but not until after the local president had made it look as though the company was really not to be trusted. He used a lot stronger language than that.

(6) It is not so much that they win loyalty for the union, but that they do it by developing antagonisms; playing up exploitive features of employer's behaviour and functions; wanting credit for everything, even when it is management's own idea; keeping management from doing anything unilaterally for the men; unseating management in its role of protector of workers' welfare.

(7) So many of the appeals, activities, and attitudes are colored by value to the *movement.* Business men are used to dealing with other business men on a business basis and are puzzled by this point of view of the union, and at times they resent the degree of solidarity that it generates in the men.

(8) During the depression we spent $20,000,000 taking care of them. Then they joined the union and asked for more, which we felt was a slap in the face.

(9) They use single events as symbols. We have made our mistakes which we would like to forget, but they live on in the minds of men. They would slowly be forgotten if the union didn't fan them into white heat every so often in order to prove to the men that they need a union. We had lots of benefits before the

union ever came along; but now they want to participate in the initiation and direction of these benefits.

(10) The union can't help but reduce the loyalty of the men to the company. Why? Let me give you a half a dozen good reasons.

They inevitably must have a split loyalty since, however good the relations are between the union and the company, they are opposed on issues and specific wage adjustments.

Even local officers, but more especially district and international officers, play up the antagonisms as means of developing loyalty to the union. You can't imagine a union developing group solidarity by emphasizing all the time what a swell company this is.

Usually it is the men with gripes, big or small, who get in first and set the tone of the union practice and attitude.

The union attitude is based on an assumption of antagonism of interest. Otherwise why have a union?

Management of twenty-five to fifty years ago built this picture of the exploiting, union-busting employer. It was accurate. That picture still colors present day attitudes. It is inevitable that union leaders make this assumption or if they don't they still feel they have to watch the employer.

They feel a necessity of stirring up or emphasizing trouble in order to prove their worth. About two-thirds are easily swayed one way or another and have no particular choice as between union and company loyalty; fifteen per cent are absolutely company men; fifteen per cent are malcontents and anti-company.

Union leaders don't really "know" management as individuals. They know management only as bargainers and sometimes do not know the ones who really make policy at that. It is easy to distrust and picture as a devil someone you don't know. Along the same line, one of the reasons that management doesn't trust the union leaders is that they don't know them.

(11) As necessary and essential as it is that the basic labor law of the land be impartial in its application to labor and management, an even more important reason for requiring legal responsibility on the part of union representatives is that the present condition puts a premium on misstatements by unions and undermining of

managements with respect to their own employees, with the result that we encourage friction and dissension and make impossible that atmosphere of good will which we all agree is essential to sound employer-employee relations. Only by an even-handed application of the theory of non-interference in employee elections, only by requiring the same degree of responsibility for its statements from the union as is now required from the employer, can the best welfare of the employees and the business be attained. Only by such impartial legislation and administration can we arrive at the goal of an atmosphere of good will.

On the other hand, the union spokesman usually considers his function to be to promote the welfare of the employees rather than that of the business. I am assuming a sincere labor leader who is truly interested in the employees' welfare. Sometimes the immediate interests of the employees is inconsistent with the long-range welfare of the business.

One unfortunate aspect in the recent development of labor organizations has been the tendency of union leaders to fall into the habit of attacking management as a means of rallying union members to the union cause.

Such attacks frequently take the direction of ridiculing management, charging management with performing acts that management has not done, or more frequently, attributing false motives to management's actions. One example of ridiculing management is a union leaflet which has recently come into my hands in which the general manager of the company is referred to as "twiddling, twirping Twining." In other cases, constructive measures taken for improvement of working conditions have been attacked as veiled methods of undermining the union. In still other cases managements have been attacked on grounds which were entirely imaginary. Tactics of this sort make an atmosphere of good will well-nigh impossible, and strike at the root of constructive collective bargaining.

Entrance of a Third Party and Injection of Irrelevant Issues Into the Firm's Industrial Relations

(1) We seem to have lost track entirely of the fact that unions and employees are not identical and that unionism and the interest

of employees as individuals are not necessarily the same. Especially is this so in the case of a union led by an irresponsible minority which uses the union to achieve its own purposes.

(2) When I took over, international officers had never been in the plant. Yet they were talking about conditions which they knew only second hand and by hearsay. I'll say this though, that it only took an invitation from me and they came and got a first-hand picture of the lay-out.

(3 The basic problem is that management is having to share policy and operational decisions with a third party, whose responsibility is first of all to an organization and membership with interests quite irrelevant to effective, efficient, and profitable operation of the business.

As it looks to top management, this working in of another partner along with interests of stockholders, employees, customers, public, and inserting a new problem for management along with controlling production, sales, etc. are not new and insuperable problems technically and organizationally. The particular difficulty lies in the nature of the interests and forces which shape the attitude and practice of this other party, and the lack of control over it.

Now regarding that first point. Remember this is a political organization and a young one. Men have to stand for election every year or so. (Could I be responsible and farsighted under those conditions?) Actually their political power depends not so much on widespread mass support as on their political ability to make alliances with political factions. These rise and fall, and the result is that we have a shifting group with which to deal. Now in political maneuvering, issues become not problems to solve between company and workers, but opportunities to make political progress within the union.

Furthermore they have the problem of holding the mass. There's a well known principle of group psychology, they are moved by sentiments and psychological reactions of the lowest common denominator. Add to this that at meetings the least responsible show up, unless there is a major issue to be decided.

One way is deliberate stirring up of hatred, showing up the boss, not only by dishonest reporting but by imputing to him the bad qualities and practices of all bosses everywhere. That destroys the basis of confidence without which no reasonable solution is possible.

An encouraging factor, of course, is the attempt by leaders to be fair. But they've raised the whirlwind in organizing and it's hard now to say, "Boys, this picture of the boss was all right as long as we were organizing, but now we're on the inside, remember it was exaggerated. He's a pretty good fellow and wants to do the right thing." That'll come if we deserve it but we'll deserve it before it comes. Because memories are long, we are paying the price of our predecessors' dumbness in fighting. We're labelled as fighters and nothing else.

Another internal factor is that where there is not complete political confusion, there are often factions with party lines which are quite irrelevant to our problems. Now if we are aware of those, we can take them into our calculations. But becoming aware of them comes perilously close to interference in internal affairs of the union. We shouldn't *interfere,* but it is difficult to deal intelligently with the matter unless one *understands* what real purpose is being served by a demand.

Now take the second point. We have internal squabbles between our own management leaders too, personal ambitions, and selfishness to deal with. But we can control that and manage it because if it interferes with company interest or is inconsistent, we can fire the man. We can't do that with the union and its leaders.

Who comes up from committeemen in the union has no necessary relevance to the real problems of the business.

(4) The thing that really disturbs us is the incomprehensible and uncontrollable maneuverings within the union itself which determine what stand they will take. We could discuss matters on common ground if welfare of the men was the issue. But the welfare of the union and the successful promotion of the interests of the union leaders seem to be the first consideration with them. We are powerless to do anything but resist that. Then our resistance is interpreted, not as good judgment but as anti-worker and sometimes anti-union. Our job is to build machines, not the union.

(5) Interests of employees and management are the same. We could make some progress in getting this across if we were unfettered by the necessity of dealing with the union. But the interests of management and the union are not the same and very often the interests of the union and the men are not the same.

(6) We worked for years to eliminate chance in our operations —now here it comes back in a big way. A new and unpredictable element has been injected into our business.

(7) It's the incomprehensible character of their objectives. Take this $2.00—this 30%—it has no relevance to a particular company's problems. Maybe it is to get the government in. Maybe it is to hold their own members. Actually there's nothing to bargain about because no settlement within the power of management could come out with the desired solution from the union's angle.

(8) The problem of getting mixed up with matters that have nothing to do with the welfare of the business enters in another way. The most reasonable, valuable, and incidentally, quantitatively greatest work of grievance men and other officers of the union is cooperation in bringing to the attention of management situations which should be corrected so that they will not result in grievances. That is business-like, fair, and reasonable. But are these gains credited to the account of the union leaders at election time? No! Only the grievances that come out in the open as disputes.

Here are some other examples of extra-firm objectives of the union:

Industry-wide bargaining.
Industrial Councils.
Statement of an auto workers' leader, "Never let the auto industry go back to competition in wages."
Efforts to evolve a proletarian political party.
Union leaders don't know where they are going except the process takes them to power.

Management is worried about the way these issues and objectives get into collective bargaining, but they have several hopes: that this Syndicalist concept of crossing plant lines in the development of interest and power will cause the union to splinter; that the common sense of their employees and their interest in the business will resist the movement; and that employer solidarity in never giving in on anything which jeopardizes the institution of their company and of management will prove an effective counter measure.

(9) There are peculiar problems which management faces in having a union in the situation. These problems grow out of the fact that although the union is actually participating in management functions, management itself has no control over the kinds of considerations that they [the union] inject into the bargaining. For instance, there are a lot of big-idea men in the union. They have been given a lot of play during the war. They have been given prestige and respect. Their counsel has been sought. They have gotten the idea that they are big shots and that what they think about the national economy and the country in general is worth listening to. They go off writing these big ideas on economics and manipulate the bargaining to bolster up these ideas. Then there is the internal maneuvering and jockeying for position within the union itself, which influences what they will demand and when they will demand it and how they will react to your counter-proposal.

There is the new experience of having a comprehensive order from the International which often-times breaks up local negotiations.

Now we recognize that the big job of the union is building itself in the early stages, but we had a hope that that would iron out after a while. But there is no sign that that is working out that way and those who know the internal politics of the union despair of any progress. It looks as though we are going to have to deal with an incomprehensible and uncontrollable third party from here on out.

One other point along this same line. From all indications it looks to me as though labor is trying to be the dominant class and that union tactics are geared to this end. Our basic job, so far as the union is concerned, is bargaining within the frame of reference of industrial relations within our company. Collective bargaining, so far as we are concerned, must be built on that premise but this objective of becoming the dominant class seems to override that.

What are they driving toward? A new class domination of America? A world labor movement calling the shots? They have to develop a technique of integration by conflict in order to accomplish this. That is the real meaning of the fear that unions are becoming political, the dangers of class domination, and the inconsistency of this with industrial relations in terms of the welfare of the individual firm.

(10) Jurisdictional strife is frustrating because we can do nothing about it. This is a part of the third party idea. The union in this situation is obviously not our men.

(11) Outsiders yes—but really that isn't so bad because it cuts both ways. Some of the "outsiders" are more reasonable and sensible than the local boys and have more perspective. We would have had a bad time on certain occasions if the outside boys hadn't been available.

(12) It is not "outsiders" so much as it is a third party which has its own needs and requirements and these are often irrelevant to worker-employer relations. You have thought of labor as your own employees. If you thought at all it was about them and how to satisfy them. Now you have to satisfy an organization that is not your own employees for reasons that are pertinent to the welfare of the third party, not the men. This organization stands in the middle, trying to bring *both* the men and the company to their point of view.

Use of "Unsound" Economics

(1) There's a big gap in their economics. It starts with the amount in the individual pay envelope and jumps clear across all the problems of managing and financing a profitable business to aggregates and averages for the industry or country as a whole. We live in the middle and are trying to operate that single firm profitably. Unless we can, what happens to both ends of their interest, the individual, his job and pay on the one hand and the total economy on the other?

(2) You'd think, to hear their arguments, that we didn't have any financial problems, or at least if we did, that wages didn't have anything to do with them. You'd think it didn't matter whether we made profits or not. They don't understand the part profits play in our economy.

(3) Often, there's no meeting of minds in negotiations because their economics are different from ours. Primarily we are involved in making a particular product with a particular market. We want to make it at a price that will capture as much of that market as is necessary in order to use our facilities at a maximum, that is at a capacity that will keep our profits at a maximum. When wages get into that picture, they get in as costs for the most part. Costs for *us,* which affect *our* prices, which affect *our* financial position, which affect *our* competitive position. The union's economic arguments involve living costs in general, the general distribution of wealth, and like matters. Management of a particular firm doesn't have any control over that.

When we say their economics are unsound, it doesn't mean really that their reasoning isn't proper for the country as a whole. But we in this company aren't managing the country as a whole. We're responsible for showing a profit to *our* stockholders.

(4) It is not always the difficulty of meeting this year's demand, but one of keeping things on a steady keel over a period. Once you've got wages at a particular level, they're sticky. You've got to think about the long run and the ups and downs. If we make a good profit this year, okay! But what of the years we lost money and the ones ahead when we're going to lose? They don't want to have wages fluctuate with profits except when profits are high.

(5) They have unsound economics. They don't want to think about costs. They assume the company is in a good position, "Look at the buildings, equipment, the salary the big boss gets, etc." They have absolutely no consideration of the financial problems of the company. They just assume it's a cash box out of which wages are paid and that we're trying to keep it full.

(6) They lack interest in the quality of production. This is not a union emphasis, but their interest in leisure, high pay, and fight

decreases their ability to focus on quality.

(7) We oppose the industry-wide wage as unsound economically because we have learned that it is always geared to the highest. The union has only one thing to sell, *getting more,* but they have no responsibility for the process by which the resources are produced from which they can get more.

The union doesn't realize the importance of production and that all wages come from production. The union doesn't realize the closeness of the margin because of the large element which raw material has in our costs. Actually in our business we have to depend on volume because the margin per pound is only one or two cents. It doesn't sound much when you say that a certain wage increase will only mean a difference of one cent a pound, but to management that means their margin is completely wiped out.

We try to preserve individual plant bargaining in part, of course, because we think it is economically advantageous to do that but also we have the bigger job of education of the plant managers and the local union leaders, and we find that if they have actually negotiated a contract themselves there is more responsibility on both sides in living up to it.

(8) When we criticize unions for not understanding the intricacies of production, financing, and marketing problems, it would be fair if we would recognize that some management people in these particular areas do not understand the economics of the problems of their associates in other particular fields. What is the difference? Well, they recognize the authority of the men in those fields and the precedence of their judgment, whereas the union doesn't.

(9) We do not believe ability to pay should be the measuring stick. What is there then to offer against other "irrelevant" considerations. They should be paid what they earn, as shown by a good incentive plan? It still has to be decided whether 100 points equals 100 cents or 80 cents.

(10) What does ability to pay have to do with wages any more than the price you pay for power or steel or rent? Ability to pay, by which they mean profits, is the result of management's skill in

buying these elements at a competitive price, combining them and organizing them in a way that results in a profit. I don't need to tell you, a Professor of Economics, about that, about the economic principles involved in buying the factors of production in anticipation of production. Though I will say some of you Professors talk as though you could stand a good elementary lecture on the subject.

(11) It isn't all bad that the unions keep shouting about things beyond the economics of the individual firm. Actually, since we have to meet those arguments they provide a stimulus to us to broaden our understanding of what the realities of economics are. There has been a lot of thinking done by management on these subjects, about the relationship of our firm to the total economy and about the soundness of the economy in general, and I must say that a lot of it has been the result of the irritation that the union has provided.

(12) I think a lot of us might go lazy if it weren't for the continuous demands that the union makes on us. Of course, there must be a limit on this but there is a certain degree of demanding which provides us with the necessity of looking for ways to reduce cost in other ways than through keeping wages down.

(13) Whatever you say about the soundness of the unions' economics, it seems to go down with the men. Now if we are really interested in finding out what the men think, then we should owe the union a vote of thanks for indicating to us what is on the workers' minds in the way of economic thinking. If we think it is wrong, then we can try to correct it, but you can't correct something that you don't understand thoroughly.

Irresponsible and Insincere Conduct Toward Employer

(1) Management's conception of responsibility and contract observance was illustrated by the following incident in my experience. The President called all of us together after we had signed the first contract and lectured us for an hour. He indicated that all contracts are a memo of understanding and mutual obligation. The understanding and the obligation are the reality. The company has found in all dealings with suppliers and other firms what value a

contract has. This is our first contract *with our own people,* and there is no reason why it should not work in the same manner.

(2) Take the case of X [a union leader] and the strike in a Pepsi-Cola plant by the CIO. AFL truckers were still delivering. They delivered to us. Some CIO stewards came out and drove the truck drivers out of the yard, threatening to upset their truck. The ringleaders were fired. The CIO struck. X got them back, and admitted on the radio that they were wrong. (It was embarrassing him in negotiations.) Then he came back and said, "Let's give the boys another chance." That's one reason, incidentally, why they can't participate in discipline.

(3) We have a seniority arrangement in our contract but every time it hurts a group important to the political support of the faction in power, then they come around for a special deal. Often-times there is reason in it too. But why have a contract then? We know and he knows he couldn't get approval of all the locals for that. Still he wants a special deal.

(4) Why must we have strikes before the grievance procedure is exhausted? We have never had a strike over an issue that went clear through. But we have had plenty that occur before the grievance procedure is exhausted.

(5) What kind of responsibility is this, declaring war before negotiations have even started? They are going to pick us off one at a time. They know that they would get 10% or 15% by negotiation, but no! They are going to declare war.

This "30%—pick them off" announcement might actually be a technique for getting control of hotheads, a fight for more than anything they can imagine. "Look now, boys, resolve our differences and perfect a disciplined army for this combat." This is a most charitable interpretation. If they can get that discipline, they think then they can use it for peace methods. But that's a dangerous strategy.

(6) The employer has chances to help smash the irresponsible element. He knows who they are. They come asking for the use of company trucks in a parade, say; a simple example. He could

refuse on the theory that he won't deal with radicals. Then he gets in bad with the responsible ones, for they don't know his reason and he is labelled as a close-fisted, non-cooperative, s.o.b. by the responsible as well as the irresponsible.

(7) The big problem is that you can't count on the word of the representatives; they think the contract is a one-way contract; they act as though anything is fair in love and war and they think of it as war.

There are so many nationalities that they don't understand each other. How can they keep their word? The top leaders really mean what they say, but can they control the men from the local presidents down? They have a whale of a job to do forming a responsible organization. They are in the stage where one man is as good as another. It's anarchy, really. Management couldn't do its job on such a basis. We have to hold our men responsible or out they go! But we can't do anything about the union people.

(8) Now the union becomes a partner in policy and procedure, but we cannot hold them accountable or control them. This is emphasized by the irresponsible conduct which is inevitable at this stage, because:

a. They are still in a town-meeting Democracy stage. When this doesn't work, they swing clear over to dictatorship. They haven't yet got the techniques of representative Democracy, relation of experts, mutual responsibilities of officers and citizens, etc., worked out. The result is confusion which we call irresponsibility. Sometimes it is properly defined in terms of character weakness of men we are negotiating with. But as often as not, it is a lack of institutional organization and control and regularity. Management couldn't be responsible as individuals if they were not backed by solidarity and integration of the organization of management.

b. The tendency is for the windy people and those who have little to lose and the politically minded to get control. The others are either too careless, or being comfortably situated comparatively, don't want the headaches. Management can't appoint the committee members and officers, but its attitude has a great deal to do with the kind that are appointed. We had an example of fine relations until a few years ago. It was the same union and the same people, but the reasonable committee members stopped serving because a changed management in the person of the President made it so unrewarding that they threw in the sponge. Then the devil-may-care boys took over and inside of a year the situation was stinking. It is back to normal now, but the President had to get out of industrial relations before it could be straightened out.

(9) I don't object to union officers being smart and good tacticians. I have to deal with that when I am dealing with business men. The difference is that those tactics among business men are carried on within a general code. There are certain rules of the game that I am for and that the other fellow is following. We probably couldn't write these rules down but we are conscious of them, nevertheless. Now the difficulty in dealing with the union man is that he doesn't know those rules and I guess that is what we mean by saying that he isn't responsible. The consequence is that many of us can see in the union only unpredictable and irresponsible action. That action may be perfectly logical and according to Hoyle, if Hoyle is defined in terms of their own codes, but the two Hoyles, that of the union man and that of the business man, are different. That is where a lot of our misunderstanding arises.

The union can't accept the fact that you are willing to accept them. There are too many memories, and the necessity for you putting up propositions opposing their demands that have nothing to do with undermining the union or exploiting the men are nevertheless interpreted in such terms.

(10) Much of what we mean by irresponsibility is just lack of power of the leaders to get all the men to accept the policy and rules as determined. For instance, there is a lack of participation by local men both of the company and of the union because the negotiations are carried on by the central office people. This means that the local people are not educated in the real meaning of the contract by actually having worked it out. Both unions and the companies have got to give more thought to real local participation. (The union official with which this company deals said the same thing.)

(11) Strikes are only one form of irresponsible restriction of output. Other forms of restriction of output are (a) paced production on the part of a group of employees in order to raise incentive rates or enforce other demands on the employer; (b) featherbedding rules resulting in unnecessary work or unnecessary workers; (c) deals with the employer that clearly restrain trade; and (d) standing in the way of technical improvements.

(12) Unions are not good for management. It interrupts our efficiency to have to be in a constant state of defense against the threat of the use of force. We have to divert management and men from their real jobs of production to straighten out difficulties between management and the union. You would be surprised at the amount of money we have paid to union men and management just to straighten out these difficulties with no relevancy of such payments to the operation of our productive machinery.

We are constantly harassed in the development of every new process and new product because we meet suspicion and antagonism to every development. We could make lots more money on them if we could move fast, but having to negotiate with the union slows us up. Moreover, we have to compromise with our best judgment in order to get things done. In negotiations, after the first meeting we have to have three or four days of cooling off in order to get down to business. The union lacks stability; after you have made a deal, you can't be sure they can carry it through. The union is not a natural, men are still individuals, they don't want to belong to groups, and if they do it is because they are forced or because they are influenced because of the conflict to stick together. If the union doesn't fight, it doesn't win.

(13) A lot of what we call irresponsibility is probably perfectly legitimate internal politics, but what it means is that influence within the union is constantly shifting. We get used to some men and they get used to us and then presto! there is a political upset in the union and we have to get acquainted with a new bunch. There is always an element in the union that think you have to have hell popping all the time or you are not doing a good job. There is no use thinking you could eliminate those boys because

others would turn up. When you couple that with the fact that the committeemen have to go back and get authority for what has been decided upon, you have got a ticklish situation and what can you say when they come back with the word, "We can't do anything with the men." Sometimes I think that the real problem of responsibility is that there is too much democracy in the unions.

(14) One thing that ought to be remembered is that we are doing pretty well, so far as negotiating and living up to the original contract. It is the supplementary agreements that cause the difficulty. That is the thing which raises trouble when we have to make a specific deal about something that wasn't covered in the contract. Sometimes we have to make it quick. The officers agree to it and then the men won't back them up. For instance, we had a strike on here at the plant. The union didn't want to strike all our plants, but we make certain parts here that are essential to the operation of all of the rest. So we made a deal with the union officers to make those parts and keep the other plants in operation. The deal was mutually beneficial but there were some hotheads in the union who were running the picket lines that kicked over the traces. To them a strike was a strike, and it wasn't good unless the plant was completely shut down. They acted in a perfectly responsible fashion, provided you accept their major premise, but it wasn't business-like just the same.

(15) One of the difficulties that we call lack of responsibility is that the union has democracy at the wrong points. It is different in management. In management we have democracy before we decide on a policy and make a contract. From then on out everybody obeys orders but the union is always trying to satisfy everybody, even after the deal has been made.

(16) I don't think the big problem is responsibility as we have defined it. Actually the problem is that the democratic procedures and the political procedures within the union have not been well worked out and because they haven't been, we can't count on what will happen, and we have no control over what will happen. Unions are making the same mistake that management made originally in their organization. They have got to the place, just like many man-

agements got to it, where they are too big to determine major policies by individual voting, but they are still trying to do that and the result is confusion; and the thing we call confusion is a large part of what is meant by lack of responsibility.

Management has one fault, just like union leaders. They tend to color any particular union by what they have heard of unions in general. We swallow Pegler's articles and other tirades. We object to their building pictures of us from a composite of what all employers are like but we do the same thing with reference to them.

(17) Parenthetically, it is rather interesting to note that while various labor groups have been vociferous in advocating management policies of nondiscrimination with respect to race, creed, color, and sex, they are unwilling to live by their own precepts and to extend the policy of nondiscrimination to include union status. The advocates of maintenance of membership, preferential shop, union shop, and closed shop apparently see no inconsistency between their advocacy of one kind of nondiscrimination while insisting on discrimination in another field.

(18) I've made out a pretty black case on union irresponsibility, haven't I? Now I've got an admission to make. I think I'm partly to blame. I'll tell you why. If you talk to X [a competitor in the same city] he'll give you a different story. He thinks the union officers of Local — are swell. "Real business-like and their word is as good as their bond," he says. Now here's the point. They are the same fellows that I deal with. X is no softy either. He's a two-fisted straight-from-the-shoulder, hard-headed business man.

(19) You know if you just read the newspapers you'd think this nation was filled with law-breaking people, because that is news. It's something like that in the union field. The irresponsible actions are news. But do you ever hear of the cases where unions and companies have lived together in the best of relations for years?

(20) When I think of the early days of business, some of the men I know about look like swashbuckling pirates to me. I know one or two that haven't been made to walk the plank yet. Now that's no excuse for them or for their counterpart in unions which

are a lot younger than business. But it does give you some hope that if business men could develop a code of square dealing, the union leaders can too. And don't forget that if I were to generalize from my own experience I'd say that the union I deal with and its officers are as responsible as any firm I've ever dealt with.

(21) There's a lot of historical accident about it I suppose. We've been lucky. I'd trust our local officers and the international to the limit. They've proved they deserve it. But if we'd had some to deal with I might be singing a different song.

(22) What surprises me is not the number of irresponsible fellows, but the number of responsible ones. When you consider the job of organizing and disciplining a half million men in the — union by leaders that aren't more than a few years off the shop floor; when you consider that most of them are not more than ten years from a knock-down and drag-out fight with the same managements who now criticize them for being unbusiness-like, why I say they've shown a lot of progress in a short time. What some can do, others can and will IF they are rewarded for being business-like and responsible.

(23) There is this much to be said for the unions. There are some signs that they are developing a solid organization, involving rules defining the relationship of the leaders to the rank and file, which promises to give us eventually the kind of an organization that we can count on; not only are such organization and rules necessary in order to have an effective union but it is a prerequisite to have responsible action under law. We may have to wait for some time until this development takes place but there are definite signs that it is on the way.

(24) One of the chief difficulties of the union is the lack of group support behind the decisions which their leaders make. They have got to have that before the leaders can really deliver. I sometimes comfort myself with the thought that some of the tactics they are using at present, which are so objectionable, may be the result of this need to develop group support and when they get that, there will be no more need for these particular tactics.

(25) You can look at these union accusations from a number of angles. One is to resent them and get sore because they are not true. Another is to study them and find out what kinds of things it is that management does which provides the union with the material which can stir the men up to militant action.

(26) I will say this, that the top union officials that I have dealt with are the biggest influence for converting the local people to the need for responsible action. I know of some of the ways in which they are trying to train their local people and the spirit in which that training is done, and I have confidence that in the long run it will be a good thing to have more than local organization because it brings to bear on the local leadership more broad-gauged and level-headed thinking.

(27) The problem of responsibility cannot be understood without realizing that the union has to work the radicals and malcontents into the solution; for these boys can bust the union if they are not satisfied. The responsible ones are not as vocal or as active.

(28) I don't know of any union leader in a responsible position who has not developed, over a period of time, capacity for responsible action. I have seen a lot of radicals changed into very reasonable fellows when they got responsibility. Maybe this doesn't always happen but it has happened in my experience. It is too much to expect that over night this kind of thing would happen, but given time, that is the direction in which things are going.

IV

UNION LEADERS LOOK AT MANAGEMENT

THE significant thing about the response of leaders of labor to my question, "What attitudes, practices, and policies of management provide you with your greatest difficulties in collective bargaining and in maintaining your unions?" is this. The areas of difficulty corresponded in almost every case to those areas designated by management.

Again it should be said that although the general character of the difficulties was verified in the responses of over sixty thoughtful labor leaders in major industrial centers of the country, the specific examples are not found in the experience of every one of them. And it may be wise to remind the reader that the analytical summary given below is a true report of reactions of labor leaders themselves and carries with it no conclusions or moral judgment as to management practice on my part. The immediate purpose is to identify and recognize the conception, on the part of labor leaders, of the problems they face in dealing with management.

The statement of the problem in each case is developed in three ways. Examples are given of the sort of experiences union leaders have had with management which illustrate the nature of the problem. Then are indicated the assumptions which union leaders believe management makes in carrying on practices which are at the root of the difficulties. Finally under the heading of "Favorable Factors" are listed some of the experiences of union leaders which seem to them to indicate possibilities for the eventual solution of the problem.

The summary of the chief difficulties in dealing with management from the point of view of the labor leaders follows.

Resistance to Increasing the Area of Terms and Conditions of Employment Determined Collectively

Examples

Attempts to retain as much individual dealings with employees as possible in such matters as merit rewards, hiring, promotions, lay-offs, grievance settlement, etc.

Insistence on the right of the individual workers to settle grievances at the first stage without the presence of a union official.

Insistence on ultimate management discretion in the disposition of grievances.

Opposition to a "common rule" in such matters as seniority, automatic progression, division of work, etc.

Utilization of piecework systems to reestablish individual rewards and punishments.

Refusal to bargain on certain items considered management's province and prerogatives, such as discipline, piece rate setting, work allocation, distribution of profits, managerial and technological innovations.

Assumptions

Management has a fundamental right to run the business in its own way, particularly in certain areas where the union should have no voice.

If the unions are given an inch, they will take a mile. Their ultimate goal is to run the business.

All individual employees should have free access to and right to deal individually with management.

Favorable Factors

Increasing willingness of management to permit submission of objections to their decisions to the grievance procedure.

Increasing tendency to consult with the union before alteration of management policy and practice.

Some pronouncements and practice indicating awareness on part of management of values in full scale collaboration with unions in areas of managerial function formerly considered the exclusive province of management.

Examples of the ability of some managements to live successfully with collaborative techniques even after violent opposition to initial demands for union participation.

Winning Loyalty Toward the Company, Often at the Expense of the Union

Examples

Unilateral innovations beneficial to the workers.

Public and private pronouncements reducing confidence in the union, antagonistic utterances discrediting union leadership, emphasis on coercive, racketeering, and trouble-making features of unions rather than on their values.

Assumptions

The company and the unions are in competition for the "loyalty" of the workers.

Management is the real promoter of workers' welfare, even to the point of protecting them from the union.

Management "knows" the workers better than union leaders do.

Loyalty to the union is an impediment to genuine usefulness of workers to the company.

Favorable Factors

Management interest in workers' welfare even with "loyalty development" as a motive provides a state of mind favorable to its improvement in cooperation with the union.

Loyalty to the company is psychologically satisfying to workers and can strengthen their confidence in the union if the latter demonstrates a genuine concern for the company's interest.

The "competition-for-loyalty" issue is more characteristic of the early conflict and adjustment stage and tends to become less important as the union leaders and management develop mutual understanding and trust.

Dealing with the Union as an "Outsider," a Third Party, and Not as an Integral Part of the Enterprise

Examples

Refusal to accept or improve union building and protective clauses such as the union shop and check-off.

Public pronouncements depicting the union as a troublesome outsider disturbing satisfactory management-employee relations.

Attitude in negotiations that union should have to prove its value to men as a basis for recruiting, and that in its success or failure management has no concern.

Hidden but effective discrimination against union members in hiring, firing, promotion, job allocations, and grievance settlement.

Union breaking and weakening tactics of all sorts.

(Note: Although few accusations were made of open antagonism and overt actions implementing it, there were many complaints of indifference toward union success and of management satisfaction when events conspired to weaken the hold of the union on employees.)

Assumptions

The union is a third party whose interests often conflict with those of the workers; in such cases the union will further its own interests.

Union leaders are primarily interested in building the union and in their own careers, only secondarily in the men.

Management's real relations are with its workers of whose interests the union gives a very imperfect reflection.

Management has no interest in the development of a strong union.

The union is a private club and not an integral part of the enterprise.

If it weren't for the union, management and workers would get along very well together.

Interests of the employees and the company are the same, but those of the union and the company are antagonistic.

Favorable Factors

Willingness of some companies to recognize the union's need for strength and to cooperate with union leaders in maintaining it.

Pronouncements indicating values of the union shop.

Widespread commitment to collective bargaining as a permanent policy.

Initiative on part of some managements in seeking out union advice and cooperation on operational problems.

Growth of union-management cooperation arrangements.

Attempts on the part of some managements to get to know the union leaders personally and to understand their problems.

Use of "Narrow" Economics

Examples

Focus on cost considerations in wage negotiations and lack of perspective with respect to the relation of earnings to purchasing power and of this to the health of the whole economy.

Resistance to sharing results of increased productivity with workers.

Refusal to consider profits as basis for wage determination.

Resistance to bargaining in industry-wide terms.

Resistance to government participation in the provision of more adequate social security and compensatory employment plans.

Failure to consider the relation of earnings to the maintenance and improvement of human resources for the firm and for the nation.

Alteration of incentive rates if workers make "too much."

Assumptions

What is good economically and from the point of view of profits for *this* firm is good for workers and for the economy as a whole.

Economic considerations are bounded by the economic welfare of *this* firm.

Distribution of the rewards of production is management's business.

Labor is simply a functional element in production or a commodity rather than human beings with personal, family, and community responsibilities and ambitions.

There is a "proper" wage for labor.

Labor is a factor of production to be bought at a competitive rate regardless of the earnings of the company.

Favorable Factors

Pronouncements of individual employers and associations of employers indicating a recognition of the relationship of the individual firm's wage and employment policy to the health of entire economy.

Willingness of some firms to negotiate and argue their position relative to the whole industry.

Articles in management journals indicating growing awareness of broader economic considerations.

Stimulus to union leadership to take account of the individual firm's cost problems.

Irresponsible and Unreasonable Attitude and Conduct of Management Toward the Union

Examples

Insistence on inability to pay as a basis of wage determination coupled with unwillingness to demonstrate by opening books.

Rigging figures or incomplete emphasis in setting forth the firm's financial condition.

Opposition to union demands "on principle" rather than on pragmatic merits.

Threats of going out of business, shutting down departments, etc. or of moving production to a lower wage area.

Chiseling on the contract, especially that initiated by legal advisors. Utilization of legal loopholes in the contract.

Provocation of work stoppages by failure to settle grievances.

Settlement of only those grievances which the company thinks it can't win in arbitration.

Lack of control of the junior supervisory force in line with the policy and commitments of top management.

Failure to educate or control junior supervisors and even plant managers in their responsibilities toward the union and the trade agreement.

Assumptions

Union should accept management's word as to financial ability at face value. Union has no right to demand a demonstration of validity of statements.

Management's "responsibility" is to stockholders for showing a profit.

"Sharp business" in dealing with the union is justified.

Legality is a sound and comprehensive basis for responsibility in human relations, particularly in relations with a union.

Favorable Factors

Genuine adherence by some managements to the spirit as well as to the letter of contracts.

Management educational programs for junior supervisors and executives.

Discipline of juniors who violate company policy.

Willingness on part of some managements to modify the contract in the light of actual problems faced by the union.

It is not bad for the union to be held to strict interpretation of contracts. It is good education and discipline.

Allegations of and Attacks on Union Irresponsibility

Examples

Public statements concerning prevalence of and dangers in union irresponsibility, racketeering, and coercion.

Advising unions how they should conduct their internal affairs.

Political activity looking toward control of unions' internal affairs.

Attempts to make unions legally responsible and limiting their resort to force.

Assumptions

Union responsibility is primarily responsibility to the company.

Employers are the guardians of the workers' and the public's interest in those matters.

Bargaining should be completely business-like with no coercion from any source. Parties should be satisfied with what can be won without force.

Favorable Factors

Irresponsible unions and irresponsible elements in all unions give the movement a black eye. Public opinion and public control aroused by employer statements, although apparently negative, may relieve the movement of embarrassing elements.

The public opinion engendered by management blasts may strengthen the hand of responsible leadership in efforts to get control.

If these attitudes and actions lead to the development of alternatives to force which works, the workers and unions will profit because force is always a dangerous weapon which may turn upon those who use it.

The biggest union problem is internal discipline, and whatever promotes that is an aid to union solidarity.

Collective bargaining is in large part a business transaction and unions have to develop business-like procedures and attitudes. Some management reactions indicate the path to that development.

V

UNION LEADERS SPEAK FOR THEMSELVES

A FEW typical quotations from the comments made by union leaders will indicate the realistic problems which they face in their dealings with management. The above analytical summary provides the overall pattern of labor reaction to management policy and practice. The quotations below are selected as representative of the varying points of view of labor leaders and of their reactions to the several difficulties.

Resistance to Increasing the Area of Terms and Conditions of Employment Determined Collectively

(1) It looks to me as though the employers I deal with are trying to keep as much of their dealings with employees as they can on an individual basis. They try to fix it so the earnings that employees get are geared to individual merit; they try to promote men on the basis of differences in individual productivity, and they try to make layoffs on the same basis. Now that all looks very good from the point of view of management, and I can understand it when you consider the kind of a job that they have; but the fact is that when they are able to do such things they can undercut the uniform standards and rules that we have been able to set up by collective bargaining; consequently we have to keep our eyes pretty sharply on such matters.

(2) Why do you suppose that they insist on the right of any individual worker to settle grievances at the first stage of the grievance procedure without the steward present? Now let me be frank about it, there are many grievances which do not involve the union or the common interests of the men. On the other hand you can never tell when an individual grievance, or rather the settlement of an individual grievance, might involve an issue which would completely upset some arrangement we've worked damned hard to get. It seems to me, therefore, that the only sensible way is to have the steward present.

(3) The big problem in this industry is rate setting. There is a general suspicion on the part of the men that every time a rate is changed it is done to cut the men's take-home. Now that isn't always true, particularly in our industry. Of course, the boss wants to reduce unit costs. The really important thing about complete management discretion over rate setting is that it retains a form of individual wages. The incentive system is used to put individual bargaining back in the picture. In spite of the fact that we have base rates and guarantees, the amount received is an amount determined for the individual and not the group. It is almost a foregone conclusion that the men cannot understand the complications of the incentive rate system; all they know is what they get. It is very hard for the union men to understand it; since they do not understand it, there is suspicion that incentive rates will be manipulated so as to establish a new effective rate outside of collective bargaining.

Another example of resistance to settling more things collectively is refusal to have the union present at the first step in the grievance procedure. This could obviously be a means of discrimination since the individual without the union representative present might get his settled immediately, whereas the one with the union representative present would have to carry his through the several steps. This has happened, although it is not a general practice; but it is one thing we have to watch out for.

(4) The most important part of our relationships with management is the grievance procedure, and I will tell you why. The grievance settlements are actually the decisions which determine what the law in the plant is. Now when the employer insists on his ultimate discretion in deciding grievances, that is a sure indication to us that he wants to lay down the law and be able to make settlements according to his own ideas for each individual rather than to abide by a rule that is the same for all.

(5) There is a sure fire sign whenever an employer wants to settle things on an individual basis. He opposes such rules as seniority, automatic progression, equal division of work, and like rules. I can see his problem so far as rewarding the most efficient

man is concerned, but we also have the problem of seeing to it that he doesn't make use of these differences in order to set up competition between the men. We are trying to eliminate that. We can't have men competing with each other and control the terms under which they work.

(6) I suppose there are some things which management has got to hold on to for itself, but it is very difficult to be sure what these are when you think of the things that they talk about such as discipline, piece rate setting, allocation of work, etc. You can see that having their own way in each of these things could be used to undermine the principle which is absolutely essential for us. If they have absolute sway in such matters, why it's harder to develop a union in which men think of themselves as members of a group rather than as individuals.

(7) It's just no use to deny that if employers had their own way and we had ours, we'd not be able to agree on one point. They want freedom, and it's our job to restrict that freedom. That's why we're in business. It's our chief reason for being in the picture. We come to some compromise on how far each can go because we've got to. The boss has his job to do and we can't do it for him, and he's got to have enough free rope to work with. But if he starts using that slack to start whipping the rope around in a way that hurts the union or the men, why we just have to shorten it up a bit. But there's no getting around the fact that unions and employers are pushing in different directions on this freedom for management business.

(8) Every time we agree on some arrangement, we've gone into some affair that management used to settle its own way. They don't like that. Don't know as I blame them. But that isn't the point. It's our job to get a voice in whatever affects the men or builds up our own strength as a union. We can usually make a deal unless management gets stubborn about its so-called prerogatives, and most of them do in one way or another. Then the sparks are apt to fly.

(9) There are very few bright lights in this picture. One of them is that some managements seem to be willing to increase

those matters which they are willing to have submitted to the grievance machinery. That is a good sign, and particularly it is a good sign when they are willing to have the grievance procedure end in arbitration, because through the third party we have another means of getting uniform rules and interpretations introduced.

One other good sign that indicates to me that management is making progress on this point is that some of them show a tendency to consult with the union before they make any major change in their policy and practice, even when this would have no effect upon the rules we hammered out collectively. That shows that they are beginning to realize the importance of making the terms of employment orderly and regular in consultation with the union.

(10) Don't forget one thing, there are a lot of managements that have continuously opposed collective bargaining and have insisted with the best of them on the right to bargain individually with their own employees. We have had to force some of them to change their tune. The encouraging thing is that after they are forced to do so, they have been able to live successfully with the deal they made, and some of them have even come out in the open and said that it is better to have a set of established rules than to try to make up the rules as they went along as each case arose. Of course I think many of them would prefer to be absolute boss in such matters.

(11) Don't forget that management itself has found the necessity of setting up rules which apply to all employees alike. Very few managements any longer deal with each situation as it arises. They have published rule books; they have industrial relations departments; they have personnel departments; and all of this means that they themselves have recognized the necessity for treating all employees alike and making it known to their employees what the rules are.

Winning Loyalty for the Company Often at the Expense of the Union

(1) The company says, when the union wins an election, "We lost the election." Now what kind of an attitude is that? It certainly shows that they believe that men can't join the union and at the

same time be loyal to the company. It is a challenge to the workers' intelligence when the company says that they know more about the needs and desires of the men than the union representatives do, and that therefore the men should put their confidence in the company instead of the union.

(2) Now look, don't get me wrong. There are lots of companies that have a real genuine interest in their men and they are constantly thinking of new ways to make their work more secure and their conditions better. Long before the union came in they worked out all kinds of benefit schemes. But others get an interest in that sort of thing only after the union gets a hold. What is the inference, I ask you, unless they do those things in collaboration with the union? The inference is this, "Look, men, you don't have to have a union in order to get these benefits, the company will take care of you." Even those that have a long record in benefit programs may have something like that in mind. We know a lot of them started on that road back in the 20's in order to keep the unions out.

(3) If they aren't really trying to show off how good the company is in comparison with the union, why don't they work out those pension schemes and the like with us? Sure, we're after credit. But that don't need to detract any from the company's good reputation, does it?

(4) There's a lot of companies that take the position that a fellow is either "our" man or a union man. You can't serve God and Caesar is the way they look at it. There is something to that if we're at each other's throats. We've done our share of playing up the worst in the employers in order to prove to the men that they need a union. So I suppose we shouldn't object when they use the same tactics on us, talking in public about racketeering, intimidation, financial dishonesty, and the like. It looks as though they're trying to make us out as black as possible in order that the worker will say, "I can trust the company more than these guys who run the unions." Sure we did the same thing in reverse, but that doesn't keep such employer tactics from being one of my headaches.

(5) It's hard to put your finger on the difficulty I have in mind but I'll try. You see a union is a part of a movement. When we get men into the union we're not just asking them to join the X club that deals with the X company. Their loyalty to the union is in part a result of what they think we can do for them as men that work for X company all right. But if they are going to be real union men, why they have got to think of themselves as a part of the movement. They have got to feel tied up with the whole story of the workingman's struggle. Now I can see why employers resent this in a way, because they may not be like the employers who were involved in this struggle. So they feel that they've got a job of holding their workers' interest and loyalty against the pull of the movement. As long as they try to do that by giving the men a better break than they could expect from most companies, I don't see any objection unless they do it in such a way as to make the men say, "We don't need a union around this place." But when they tar us with all the skullduggery that's gone on in the movement from the beginning of time so that men will steer clear of us, why that's a horse of a different color.

(6) It isn't all bad though, this unilateral benefit stuff. A company can't go for that without learning a lot about the needs of the men, and if the union is on its toes it can profit in its negotiations from that increased understanding. If we are sensible, we can demonstrate over a period of time the value of our participation, if we can convince the company that our primary interest is in the welfare of the men.

(7) What's wrong with the men having real confidence in and respect for and loyalty to the company? You get more kick out of working for a boss you respect and that you know wants to play square with you. If the union shows that it is also interested in improving the company and its chances, we get the benefit of that. It runs something like this in the minds of the men. "This is a swell company. I want to do my best for it. The union does too. I can do what I can better by belonging to the union."

(8) This idea that it's either you be a company man or a union man, doesn't last forever. It had to be stressed in the early organiz

ing days pretty hard. And when we had a fight to get recognized there just wasn't any two ways about it. You stuck with one or the other. But after fifteen years of dealing with this company, that idea is pretty much licked. It could come out again, I suppose, under a different management, but this one goes along with us trying to build its own reputation with the men, but at the same time realizing we have problems too; and they're grand guys in helping us to work them out.

Dealing With the Union As An Outsider, a Third Party, and Not As An Integral Part of the Enterprise

(1) The thing that gets me most is that they haven't really accepted us as we think of ourselves, that is, a real part of the enterprise. Perhaps we have been to blame for that for appearing to want to get something more out of them all the time and because it is true that a movement is something new and foreign in the operation of a business. But we aren't just a private group either. When the union gets into the plant, what it does, for better or for worse, becomes a part of the operation of that plant and it is important for the company that the union be a good solid affair.

(2) You would think that we were a private bridge club or golf club or something, the way a lot of them look at it. They act as though it didn't make any difference whether the men belonged or not. If we sell ourselves to the men they say, that's all right; if we don't, all right. It makes no difference to them. Now, it's pretty hard for us to act as a responsible part of the business when management takes that attitude.

(3) It looks to me like management would want to help build up the union by union-shop clauses and check-off, for instance, as long as they have got to deal with it. What would you say if a firm decided that they had to employ a firm of accountants but also said that they didn't care whether it was a strong or a weak firm? A part of the union's ability to be a successful part of the business depends upon its strength. Don't you think management ought to have a big interest in that?

(4) Whenever an employer talks about the union as a troublesome outsider, he may be speaking the truth about it being trouble-

some; but unions are here to stay and they are not outsiders, and they will not have real cooperative relations with management until management gets over that attitude.

(5) This idea that we are an outsider comes out in its worst form, of course, when the company tries to bust the union. The old days of union busting are gone, I hope, but there are countless ways of discriminating against union members, in hiring men and firing them and in moving them around from job to job and in grievance procedure. Whenever you see an employer using these tactics you know that he looks upon the union as he would look on a wart on the end of his nose. He may have to put up with it, but he would like to get rid of it. It don't belong there.

(6) The companies frequently take the attitude that it is none of their business to keep the men in the union and collect dues. This indicates their conception that the union exists out there by itself. It is a third party. It's pretty hard to deal with them when they follow an arm's length policy.

(7) What gets me is the reaction of some employers that if there just wasn't any union, management and the workers would get along very well together. Why do you suppose unions ever got started anyway if that was true? And if it wasn't true, and there were troubles between management and the workers that it took a union to straighten out, then the union becomes a very important part of those relations and is not just an outsider butting in.

(8) It isn't all management that take this attitude. I will say that in my experience there are an increasing number of them who seem to recognize that the union has to be strong, and they are willing to cooperate with the union leaders in making it strong. I was talking with a guy the other day who made a slip when he said, "Now, Jim, *our* union . . ." and then he caught himself. He wasn't thinking of it as a company union either or as one that he could dominate. He just meant that he had a genuine interest in its success, and I know he does.

(9) The management papers and magazines aren't as rabid as they used to be about the union, and the need to hold it at arm's length. Why, in recent months I have even seen some articles in

those sheets listing values in the union shop and the check-off, and, of course, there is a very widespread approval, even if it is only on paper, of collective bargaining as a permanent policy. Now when that really gets into their blood, I doubt if they can really keep on thinking of us as outsiders.

(10) The best indication that some managements have begun to think that we are a part of the family is that they come seeking us out for advice and help on operational problems. To be sure, that is usually the guy who is on a spot, but even if it is a last resort, it shows some development in management thinking.

(11) We haven't got many union-management cooperation contracts with the major firms in this industry but we have got quite a number with smaller companies, and they are working. There is no question in those situations about the union being an outsider. It's in there, and with both feet.

Use of "Narrow" Economics

(1) "Profits have nothing to do with wages," they say; but you will notice that that is only when profits are going up; but when profits come down then it is a different matter.

We asked the companies to bargain on an industry-wide basis. They say it just can't be done but they won't explain why. They've never given me a satisfactory answer to the question of why, since the product sells for the same all over the country, they pay different wages.

(2) We are operating on different principles in economics and over-all emphasis. The companies' economics and emphasis is workable plant by plant, company by company at the most. Our interest cuts across plants. If the company has a number of plants, we want to bargain company-wide in order to eliminate any inequalities between wages paid in different plants of the company. Our point is, if there is some advantage to the company locating in different areas because, let us say, of the cost of living, why shouldn't the workers have the benefit of that location as well as the stockholders? We want to bargain industry-wide in order to keep wages from being used as a means of competition between firms. Let 'em

compete in anything else, but not in wages, hours, and working conditions. They shouldn't be able to compete by using human beings as pawns.

(3) Of course we know that the company has to worry about costs, even if we don't know too much about the inside workings of that problem. We don't object to a company saying that they can't pay these wages because it will raise costs and because if it does they can't get the business. What we do object to is their insistence on making that the *only* point on which bargaining should rest. Why can't they get the idea that purchasing power is as important to them as low costs and that high standards of living throughout the whole economy will react to their individual benefit eventually? They can ask us to take the long view on matters. Maybe they ought to take the long view too.

(4) We don't object when they say they can't pay more because wages have to come out of production, but they don't hold to that tune when our productivity has increased. They could pay us then but they find some other reason for not doing it.

(5) The only sensible way to run these big industries is to operate some basic things like wages on an industry-wide basis. That would leave plenty of room for competition between managements on all kinds of matters. But what you would find is that so far as this one industry is concerned, one management can't get an advantage over another by taking it out of the hides of its workers. There may be other objections to industry-wide bargaining on wages, but I would like to see them come out in the open and really think it through with us and not just object to it on the basis of the right of each company to operate its own affairs in its own way.

(6) There's one thing that is pretty solid in the bosses' ideas about wages. I can see their point on this too. The way they look at it they buy labor just like they buy power or steel or floor space or what you will. I read an economic textbook once that called these the factors of production. They buy them before they have any product to sell. A few days or weeks or months later they have worked with those things so that something is put out which can

be sold. Then they get the money back that they advanced to buy those things. But the difference is that stockholders aren't paid until the books are added up, while the others are paid beforehand. So they say what the stockholders get depends on what profits we make, but what the others, including labor, get should depend on what the going rate is. I talked with a big shot from my company who said there was no more sense in paying labor according to profits than to paying for coal or light or steel or rent on that basis.

Theoretically, I suppose, that's sound economics, but it treats labor as a lifeless commodity just the same and it's a narrow point of view. The way labor acts while production is going on is a lot more important in determining what the profits will be than that bar of steel. That bar is set when you buy it, but the worker isn't. What he does and what he is worth depends a lot on whether he feels he is justly treated; and a part of that feeling is bound up with whether if the company is making good money they couldn't pay better wages. That's especially true because he knows for sure that if they don't make good money he may be in for a wage cut. It's happened, you know.

(7) There is very little to show that management as a whole has thought broadly about the economic consequences of social security and various other kinds of schemes to provide economic security and employment. They just naturally resist more government participation in such things, chiefly because it costs them taxes. You would think they never heard about such things as the human resources of a nation. A lumber firm would understand all right that it had some interest in the keeping up and improving the forest resources of this country; and so would a coal firm about coal; and an oil firm about oil. But all of them use human resources, and they don't seem to be able to see what wages have to do with that big problem or the relationship of government plans of various kinds to it.

(8) There are plenty of employers, particularly in meetings, who talk about management getting wise to itself and realizing that its selfish interest is tied up with help to the whole economy.

That's an encouraging sign. Of course, they usually wind up by coming back and saying that what is good for this firm is automatically good for the whole country, but it shows they are thinking along these lines anyway.

(9) We have found some firms that are beginning to think in industry-wide terms. You can't blame them for resisting it because it is new, at least in our part of the world, but just the same I think I can see a glimmer of light on this issue. Their arguments are getting more and more on to the ground of sensible economics and less and less on the grounds of just blind opposition to it.

(10) Of course, this unwillingness to take the broader view makes it tough for us in negotiations, but in a way I am glad that they have kept their eyes focused on the profitable operations of the individual business, because in that way us fellows in the movement have got a damned good education about cost problems of the individual company. If they hadn't stood so solid on those grounds that look to be very narrow, we wouldn't have been forced to think as thoroughly about them. So it may work out all right in the end.

Irresponsible and Unreasonable Attitude and Conduct of Management Toward the Union

(1) The thing that is really irresponsible about some bosses is that some of the positions they take don't jibe with what they are willing to do. For instance, they insist that the union shall consider the welfare of a company as primary. That is, can the company pay this bill? But in the same breath they refuse to demonstrate to us whether they can or can't, and say it is none of our business how the company spends its money. By Jove! if what we can get depends on the ability of the company to pay, and I think it does, then it looks to me like eventually we have got to have something to say about how much money there is going to be for wages, and we are certainly going to have to insist that the company demonstrate what it can and can't do. This isn't any challenge to their honesty. It is just good reasonable business procedure. Of course, you realize that we aren't without some experience with managements who contended that they weren't able to pay and then rigged

the figures or didn't give the proper emphasis to the figures they handed out as to their financial condition.

(2) The most troublesome, and I am going to say the most irresponsible, action is to oppose union demands on some principle or another. I don't object to principles, but some of them seem to be made up as they go along. I call it irresponsibility to shift ground from the actual results of a particular demand or the actual problems connected with putting it into effect and just flatly refuse to consider it because they are opposed to it "on principle."

(3) If we were irresponsible to threaten to strike, and I think in some circumstances we were, then their threats of going out of business, shutting down departments, or moving production to other towns is irresponsibility of the same sort.

(4) The chief problem in our territory isn't dealing with top management. We get along fine with them but somehow by the time their policy and decisions get down into the lower ranks of management, they don't turn out to be the same, especially when they get down to the foremen. I am all for union responsibility and for the ability of the officers to control the men, but I am telling you right now that management has got a job of responsibility too and that a lot of the trouble comes because they can't control the boys down the ladder.

(5) If there is anything that gets my goat, it is the discussion and settlement of grievances with an attitude that seems to be more interested in winning cases against the union in order to destroy its prestige than to get the matter worked out. It would seem to me that it would be the responsibility of management to try to work out the grievances, whoever won, and get the conditions right so it wouldn't happen again.

(6) I can understand his cost problem, but he won't back it with facts. I've dealt with men who argued about financial position and competition problems. Nothing there to get, they say. I can understand that. *But* only a few will lay it on the line and prove it. One did in X—. "I haven't got the dime, Mike," he says. "I trust you, Bill," I says, "but the boys don't." "What can I do to prove it?" he says. "Suppose I get a firm of C.P.A.'s which you select, will

you take their word?" I did, and sure enough he didn't have the dough. So without disclosing any information, I went to the boys and told them to lay off and get busy and we'd put that money in the till. Well, we did and six months later got our dime. But we'd have never been able to put it across unless he'd been willing to lay it on the line. Now, all companies couldn't do that or disclose plans for investment and expansion. But it would go a long way if they would trust me to understand *and* keep their confidence.

(7) One of the things that might be called management irresponsibility is the leaving of matters to their attorneys. These attorneys have to make good. We would like to have the contract made in general terms, and we always start with a rather general contract, but then as often as not we find that these attorneys, in order to make themselves useful, start chiseling; the result is that we learn every year of some new specific point that we have to nail down. I know that is bad for the company, it ties them up, and it is bad for both of us because it creates a situation in which we don't seem to trust each other. But if the companies would keep their attorneys out of it, it wouldn't happen that way so often.

Another example of irresponsible action, the grievance settlements at the early stages don't always seem to be intended to improve the situation. Those are settled which the company doesn't think it can win in an arbitration and those are not settled which the company thinks it can win in an arbitration. In other words, they seem to have their eyes on the balance sheet of the arbitrator's awards rather than on improving the situation.

The company seems suspicious at the start of all leaders. They are, of course, basing their judgment on past experience that most union leaders are hard to deal with and irresponsible from their point of view. The result is that a fellow who really wants to be a responsible, reasonable chap finds himself behind the eight ball and under the necessity of proving himself. Unless he has lots of guts and perseverance he is likely to say, "What's the use?"

(8) When I talk about irresponsible management conduct, I am not talking about striking a hard bargain. I expect that. That is what they ought to do. The most responsible men that we deal

with are hard bargainers. What I am talking about is lack of good faith and trying to pull fast ones on us.

(9) Shouting about union irresponsibility while carrying out an arm's length policy with respect to the union is bad. Any man with sense should realize you can't do business in that way. And I'm saying we're irresponsible when de do the same thing to the employers.

(10) The companies haven't always lived business-like under their contracts. They are negotiated in the central office, just like our contracts are. Then they are sent out to local management. Not all of our locals like it, not all plant managers like it. We have some problems holding our boys in line, but so do they. The local managers start chiseling. Most of our contracts don't contain elaborate wage structures. They chisel where they can on a local basis in order to reduce costs. They're all in competition for head office approval. It may not look like chiseling to them but it does to the men. In a shifting production picture they leave a lot of the boys dissatisfied on reclassifications. Now a fellow getting $1.05 on a pre-war job is shifted to a job on a government order taking nearly the same kind of work—still $1.05, then 15% = $1.20, plus $.15 = $1.35 on this job. Now we go back to peace-time. This job isn't in the contract. It gets rated at $1.05. Is that responsible action? They didn't even negotiate. Shifting production to lower paid areas is another example of irresponsibility.

(11) A lack of confidence and trust is the big stumbling block on both sides. Either one that talks or acts in a way to destroy that or to indicate to the other fellow that he wouldn't trust him behind a door with a cold potato is acting irresponsibly.

(12) The most irresponsible action of the companies is the attempt to place the responsibility or blame for bad relations on the unions without realizing the company's part in the whole affair. For instance, there is this claim that we are always using pressure and conflict as an organizing method. That is true. Right now, of course, we don't have to worry about whether we have to create conflict because we have plenty of resistance which is obvious to everybody. Why do we make big demands? Because we have

learned that industry gauges its reaction to the strength of the demand. If they want us to stop organizing, they could do that by giving us the union shop. What does it look like when a company is talking about unreasonable union action on grievances and eighty per cent of the grievances are decided in favor of the union at the umpire level?

(13) There is a growing number of firms that are really trying to administer their contracts in the spirit of cooperation instead of in legalistic terms. Now we can do something on that basis. There is another good sign and that is these educational programs for supervisors and foremen. That is where the trouble is most times, and if management can really lick that problem, they will find that a lot of unions are going to be more responsible too.

(14) Maybe this isn't good for us and maybe we ought to have to live with a particular contract that some of our unskilled people worked up. As a matter of fact, at the International office we insist on that. That is, if the men have made a bad deal, we tell them they've got to hold off until the next contract negotiation time rolls around. But there are some places where unexpected problems come up for the union because of the contract arrangements they have made and there are some managements that show a willingness to make supplementary agreements that will get over that stumbling block. The need for this, of course, will not be so great when our boys learn better how to negotiate.

(15) It is not always bad for the union to be held to a strict and even legalistic interpretation of the contract. It may be tough but it is good for us, and I would even go so far as to say that those companies that have made us toe the line have done us a lot of good in the long run.

Allegations of and Attacks on Union Irresponsibility

(1) One of the hardest things that we have to face is this constant picking at us in public by outstanding representatives of management. This isn't done much on a local basis. It isn't done too much by the individual plant management. They have to live with their boys and they know that it doesn't do much good to the relationship to be attacking unions as irresponsible, racketeering gang-

sters; but I am not too sure that the ones that keep still in public also keep still when certain more loud-mouthed people sound off in private.

We have spent altogether too much time defending ourselves against such attacks. The attack itself isn't so bad but it is the fighting attitude that shows up when those statements are made and which we know is still there that is bad. It gives the hotheads just the kind of ammunition they need. They can say "Look, you see, management really doesn't want this union. Don't be dumb. They are still fighting it." Now I say that in spite of the fact that a lot of what they point out about the unions is true. We probably have got to be controlled, and I wish to God that our own union would get busy and work out controls from the inside. But just the same it doesn't come very good from management, particularly from the ones who have long been known to be opposed to unions, to be advising us how to run our own affairs and to be promoting legislation for setting up machinery to control us in the way we operate our own affairs.

I am not objecting, either, to pressure for making unions more responsible. The hotheads and the malcontents and the just plain cockeyed guys give the movement a black eye, and if public opinion and government control can reduce those elements without busting the movement, they will relieve us of a lot of embarrassment. There is some degree also to which the public opinion that is whipped up by these blasts from management may hold up the hands of fellows like myself who believe in thoroughly responsible unions, and help us to get more control of our own affairs. The worst thing, though, is that once you get some law on the books, why the anti-union boys have another opening to bust unions in general, good with the bad. We've learned that from bitter experience.

If the kinds of controls, and particularly the kinds of substitutes for strikes which grow out of this agitation will only work, it may be that both the workers and the unions will find it to their advantage because force is always a dangerous weapon which can destroy those who use it. You know there is an old saying, "Those who take the sword will perish by the sword." That is true to a certain degree. But really what I am afraid of is that instead of helping the responsible elements and providing industrial peace machinery which really works, these attacks on the unions just emphasize the split between management, unions, and the public. They make us fighting mad, and that is a poor attitude for making any machinery work, no matter how good it is. But let me end up with this, that the biggest problem we have got in the movement today is internal discipline and if anything will help out on that problem, it will be a big advantage, not only to the movement but to business and to the public. My only hope is that we will work out the problem ourselves and not hand any clubs in the form of legal restrictions to those who want to beat us into the ground.

(2) Now here's a pretty picture for you. Did you read the blast X— let out the other day damning the unions up one side and down the other? And for why? Well, we pulled his place last week though the International is sore about it and is trying to get us back. And it's been a pretty rough affair. Some heads have been cracked including old Jake's. He's a foreman the boys would just as soon see six feet under. We broke our contract, he says. So we did. But not a damned foreman in that place ever acted like we had a contract for three years now. Don't tell me old X— doesn't know it either. What really gets me is this holier-than-thou attitude from the very guy that took no responsibility for his own gang. Then when we can't get any help through the grievance machinery, which he agreed to, and face the same old bullheaded tactics day after day till we finally have to pull the joint, then it's *us* who break our contract. We're the irresponsible guys. Some folks forget the movement is a pressure and power business and the accent is on the pressure and power. The business side of it is a method, not the guts of the organization. It's safer to follow the business way, observing contracts and all that if you can. And I for one believe the more it can be done the better off we'll be. But just like contracts aren't the only way business men go after each other to put the squeeze on, we have to use other ways too.

(3) There's no reason why employers shouldn't complain about the way our locals down in X— and Y— have acted. I've spent

more time trying to bring those boys into line than all the rest of the locals in my territory. If the whole membership behaved like they do, we wouldn't have no organization at all. But why do they have to damn the whole movement?

(4) I suppose it's natural for business men to kick when some of our boys go off the deep end and do things that was necessary in the old days when the bosses were definitely ganged up to bust the unions. But they don't seem to remember that we've got long memories. Those days weren't so long ago you know. And while they're kicking about our not knowing the meaning of contracts, they might ask themselves how long it took business men to keep their word even when it didn't pay them to do it. If you know anything about American history you'll realize how many years it took to make 'em all toe the line. Some of their ruthless deals would put the unions to shame. That's no excuse, mind you. But it might make them less impatient and keep them from being so all fired righteous-like, if they'd look back at their own record once in a while.

(5) One thing these fellows that blast the unions forget about is that it's our job to change the rules as much as it is to live up to them. Those rules didn't come down from heaven. No one sat down and figured them out. They got made because somebody thought it would be to their advantage to have them and had the power or influence to get them set up. Our interest is in the workers. They didn't have much voice in making those business rules. The result is that they work against the working class as often as not. Now we're out to change that. We've got the power to do some of the job and we need more. But when you do, you make someone mad who is well set up under the old rules. He's ready to fight to hold on to them. So you've got a struggle on your hands and sometimes a war. You always have more or less of a war if you want to compel people to do something they didn't have to do before. They say their rights are being violated. Sure they are. It's a union's job to get more rights for the worker and that usually means less for the boss. That's not a business deal though on important matters. When you are in the thick of it you just know it's different, that's

all. I say again that a big part of the union's job is to change the rules.

I started out to say that one of our biggest difficulties is this attitude that blasts us to Hell when we don't act like perfect business men, when all the time we are only doing what we have got to do if we carry out our big job. Really it isn't a proper gripe because you can't expect them to like it. You can't blame employers when the balance of power is upset and falls our way instead of theirs. But they might stop expecting us to be what we ain't.

(6) I don't really think we've got much to kick about when they say we act more like we was a fighting outfit rather than a business organization. That's been true in the past and it will be true as long as we have to fight for a decent living for our boys and for the life of the union. And the end is not in sight so far as the general picture is concerned. But what worries me is the cases where management is willing to go the whole road with us, be reasonable, and business-like and do the level best they can, not only for the men but to build up the union. We're all set up and trained to scrap for every crumb we get and our boys can't always change their tune. These employers are right guys and the more we find of them the sooner we can stop getting ready for a scrap even while we're getting along fairly well. So far as International policy is concerned you've got to remember that we've got all types of employers to deal with, not just the good ones. So maybe they're right when they say we are dominated by a fight attitude. Maybe we have to be. But it just ain't true that we'd rather be fighting than eating. Give us time and good experience from being business-like, and not being taken advantage of because we are, and we'll show them some new angles to business practice and responsibility.

VI

THE BASIC ISSUE

INDUSTRIAL warfare will plague America until leaders of labor and management understand and respect the survival needs of each other. Management has deep convictions, born of experience, about the "principles of sound management." Labor leaders have deep convictions, born of experience, about the "principles of effective unionism." Each is convinced that if he compromises his principles he encourages a threat to his own survival. Many labor leaders believe that if unions become the kind management labels "sound", they will cease to be "real" unions. Many employers believe that if management yields much more to union pressure, it will cease to be "real" management. That belief keeps both in a fighting mood basically. Each group sees in the attitudes, actions, and policy of the other a threat to its own survival.

I am not talking about physical survival. That alone isn't what men are willing to fight for in a civilized community. They will fight to preserve the familiar opportunities for reaching their goals: the respect of their fellows, economic security, control and independence, understanding, and integrity. They will fight to preserve in traditional form the kinds of organizations and institutions which provide them with those opportunities. They will fight for the privilege of continuing to act as they always have acted, in ways which their group considers effective and proper. They will fight to preserve the ideas, the symbols, the ritual which reenforce such behaviour and make it "right" in their eyes. The survival of this whole structure of living is what men mean by survival.

When that structure is threatened, they do not want peace until the threat is removed. That is the basic problem. Why? Because men will not cooperate with those whose actions, they believe, threaten their survival. They may have the skills and the brains to cooperate, but they will not use them for that purpose. Because arrangements for reducing conflicts through collective bargaining haven't a chance to succeed unless they are consistent with the jobs both management and labor leaders have to perform. Because agencies such as mediation and arbitration boards will not be used willingly and with confidence unless their activity is compatible with doing those jobs well. Because codes and laws will be resented at best and short-circuited and disobeyed at worst if they do not meet the fundamental survival needs of those whose actions are governed.

The basic issue in labor-management relations at the moment then, arises from the fact that each party is concerned primarily with its *individual* survival. Its attention is focused on the means to that end. The leaders of each group are trying in every industrial negotiation and every political maneuver not merely to solve a specific problem. They are trying to solve it in a way that preserves their own structure of living intact. They are expecting peace on terms consistent with the maintenance of their own sovereignty. Preoccupied with that expectation and the effort to implement it, they have forgotten a very fundamental truth: that sovereignty in a democracy must be shared, not exclusively possessed by a particular group. Many have neglected the fact that partnership is essential to a democratic relationship in industrial as in political and family life; and that if one would be a partner, the other partner's interest must become one's own, at least to that degree which permits cooperative effort toward a common goal.

This does not mean that the individual interests of the parties must be identical or even that there must be no conflict between them. The achievement of peace and workable arrangements in labor-management relations is not premised upon the immediate disappearance of conflict. It is not unreasonable to suggest, however, that the conflict can be conducted in an atmosphere of mutual respect without resort to the methods of open and violent warfare.

The difference in interests among workers, union leaders, and management is rooted deeply in the objectives, responsibilities, functions, and traditions of each; it arises from a difference in economic and social status to preserve or improve which the parties have developed different ways of life, supported by different philosophies, folklore, symbols, slogans, and codes. Even when they use the same words, the meaning for each differs, for the meaning is built from the facts of life which each experiences. When management, owners, union leaders, and workers use the words "wages," "production," "profits," "justice," and others, they fill the words with content that bears the mark of their own way of living. The conflict over wages, for instance, is not merely a battle over a particular rate, but a competition among three patterns of life in one of which wages are items on the cost sheet, in another are the foundation of living, and in the third are one focus of a service rendered. But such differences and conflicts need not lead inevitably to open warfare.

Peace in industrial relations is best defined, in Sumner's phrase, as a state of antagonistic cooperation. Although pursuing each his own interest, the parties recognize their mutual dependence upon each other, agree to respect the survival needs of the other, and to adjust their differences by methods which will not destroy but rather improve the opportunities of the other.

The conditions required to accomplish such a result are many and complex. In this pamphlet I have discussed only one. But I think it is basic. It is this: that each party shall understand thoroughly the kind of a job the other has to do, his convictions about what is necessary if he is to do that job well, the way in which the nature of the job and those convictions impel him to act as he does; that each shall see to it that his action, based on that understanding, does not threaten the survival of the job or the organization with which the other identifies himself.

Understanding the behaviour of the other party does not imply the necessity for approval. One need not, and probably cannot, approve all he understands. But to know why the other behaves as he does is to be armed with useful knowledge upon which intelligent action can be based. In the day-to-day development of workable relations between management and labor it is far more important for each to know *why* the other behaves as he does than to have convictions about how he *ought* to behave. The *why* in terms of the compulsions placed upon him by the nature of his job and his structure of living represents facts which are as realistic as a payroll or a power line. Knowing such facts as they are, not as one would like them to be, is the first step toward achieving industrial peace.

It is only the first step; but until it is taken, the nature and direction of further progress cannot be determined intelligently. The adjustment itself which must be made in thousands of individual circumstances is the ultimate necessity. It will test the realism of the knowledge each party has of the facts which determine the action of the other. It will demonstrate whether both really want peace consistent with those facts. It will challenge the best skills and wisdom that practical men have. It will prove whether civilized men in labor and management can supplant the techniques required for *selfsurvival* through domination with the skills and wisdom required for *mutual survival* through cooperation.

The task is hard, but not impossible. The chances for success are reflected in the satisfactory relations of thousands of managements and unions over the country. Whether or not they develop the will to succeed is not a matter of choice for union leaders who desire the survival of free unions and for management leaders who desire the survival of free management. For the result of failure to work out the means of *mutual survival* will not be the elimination of one by the other, but the elimination of both as free institutions by public regimentation. Never were the words of the sage more applicable than to all leaders of labor and management in twentieth century America, "No man liveth unto himself."

MUTUAL SURVIVAL

PART TWO

The Development of Antagonistic Cooperation, 1966

THE DEVELOPMENT OF ANTAGONISTIC COOPERATION

THE preceding section of this book was written in 1946. Collective Bargaining as a major factor in setting the tone and practice of industrial relations in most sectors of large scale industry in the United States was barely 10 years old. During nearly half of that period relations of unions with management were carried on under wartime necessities which constrained and retarded the full use by either of the parties of their power forcefully to challenge the actions of the other. The attitudes and reactions of the parties at that time were those of men who were, to be sure, learning from experience, but learning slowly, how to deal with each other, what to expect of each other, how to shape successful policies and practices of the institutions for which they were responsible under conditions in which each had to plot his course with a view to the impact of his moves on the other.

Two decades have passed since 1946, during which I have been continuously and actively involved both as an academic analyst and as a practitioner in the developing relations between management and labor orgnizations. What follows is an attempt to bring to bear the observations resulting from that experience on a reassessment of my earlier conclusions and on an evaluation of the results of the efforts of the parties toward Mutual Survival during that 20 years.*

There were plenty of obstacles to productive and peaceful labor-management relations in those years right after the War. Most of them are still with us. Some of them have been reduced in potency by the mere fact that men on both sides have learned their jobs better and have learned to work together because they *had* to work together. Some of them have been reduced by the positive initiative of inventive leaders. Some of them have been

*My first reassessment was made in 1958 and published in the *Proceedings* of the 11th Annual Meeting of the Industrial Relations Research Association. What follows is an updated and amplified adaptation of that article.

reduced by the retirement from the scene of men in management and unions whose training and predispositions were, to put it as kindly as possible, unsuited to the tasks of the moment. Many of these are now enjoying in the great beyond the rewards of their efforts here on earth.

It is fair to say that no obstacles have stood in the way of the development of a kind of collective bargaining which, I believe, provides a foundation for the straightening out of unavoidable and inevitable differences between people who work and the people they work for, which is sounder than that existing in any major country in the world.

Our sanguine optimism of 20 years ago, that the passage of time would cure many of our difficulties has, however, had to be replaced by a more realistic recognition that time is simply the framework in which what *has* happened influences what *does* happen and in which what *does* happen stimulates what *is going* to happen.

Two decades ago there seemed to me to be one obstacle to productive working relations between union and management leadership which dwarfed all the others. What was it? It was that both management and labor leaders had suddenly waked up to the fact that a basic shift was taking place in their relative power and prestige in industry and the community, and they saw every event, big and small, affecting that shift.

That fact hadn't really struck home before the War. The significance of the extraordinary growth of trade union membership in the 5 years following the Wagner Act did not, before the war, strike management as a *permanent* threat to the economic power and control they continued to exercise in areas other than the determination of wages, hours, and working conditions. It is true they were disturbed and oftentimes angry, but they were not lacking in confidence that, as one of them said to me, "The worm will turn." Labor leaders of old and young unions were still as much concerned about their power relative to each other as about their power relative to management.

Then came preoccupation with war production, and the leadership of both groups faced a common challenge. On the whole they met it in a spirit of partnership. There was plenty of disagreement, but they were concerned more with developing power *for* getting a big job done than in gaining power *over* each other.

With a return, at the close of the war, to relatively free collective bargaining and the open pitting of strength against strength, however, it became obvious that something lasting had happened in the power structure. Labor leaders had consolidated their memberships through services rendered, through organizational arrangements, through internal political machines, and through working relations with government agencies and elected officials. They had become familiar and influential people in political and governmental circles. The names of many of them were now more familiar to the man on the street than the names of prominent industrialists and businessmen. And they shared, in the public's estimation, the credit for patriotism and devoted effort in the winning of the war.

Labor leaders gave ample evidence that they were aware of, and confident in their newly won power. Wage demands for 30¢ an hour startled not only management but ordinary citizens accustomed to think of 10¢ an hour as a normal bargaining demand. "Out with maintenance of membership" was labor's cry, "We demand *real* union security, the closed or the union shop." Strikes of widespread proportions causing grave inconvenience and real hardship to the public were threatened and called, and in many cases carried through to successful but costly conclusions. At least a few outstanding and photogenic labor leaders appeared to many people to consider themselves and their unions strong enough to challenge even the United States government.

Management, supported by many startled middle-class people in cities and on the farm and their political representatives, raised the cry "Restore the balance!"

In this atmosphere the Taft Hartley Act, and, 12 years later, the Landrum-Griffin Act, were passed. In public conferences and private conversations a worried management discussed and initiated industrial relations and political strategies for *containing* or *countering* the new power of unions. This atmosphere covered the country when I wrote *Mutual Survival.* In that atmosphere no issue seemed a minor one because, in such a period of changing forces, no one could be certain what impact a small gain or loss might have upon the basic issue. And that basic issue was that both management and labor leaders appeared to the other to be attempting to accumulate or regain power and sovereignty for their own organizations in ways that threatened the power and the sovereignty of the other.

That is still the basic issue. In some ways it isn't as stubborn as it was then. But in other and important ways it is more stubborn. It is less stubborn as a personal problem of particular managers and labor leaders adjusting their self-conceptions and their personal feelings to a new relative power and prestige relationship between them. It is more stubborn as an organizational problem of particular institutions, companies and unions, adjusting their policies and practices to a developing and hardening relative power relationship between institutions. It is more stubborn because the private strategies and tactics of the parties increasingly have made their impact felt, not just on each other, but on the whole people, the public; and the public is demanding that private policy be constrained by controls and responsibilities exercised in the public interest.

Let's look at the relatively bright side of the picture first. No one who talked with management and labor leaders 20 years ago could miss the fact that in many cases they took the shift in the power situation personally. Both of them knew, and all the rest of us knew, that labor leaders had risen rapidly in their ability to influence the course of events in this country. Moreover, their gain had been accomplished at the expense of some of the power and prestige formerly possessed by management. Being an egghead at that time—I still am—I was inclined to take the long view in something like these words:

> A century and a half ago business enterprisers offered the same challenge to the landed gentry. In those days businessmen were in the saddle riding their steeds with enthusiasm toward a grand and glorious new day which their efforts were to make possible. Today labor leaders are feeling the same sense of power and promise.
>
> It is characteristic of socially, economically and politically powerful groups to interpret a decrease in their power as a personal defeat

> and a threat to the whole structure of the society. It is a characteristic of groups on the make to interpret their advances as a personal victory and a step forward in the march of progress. The result is likely to be an attitude of frustration and bitterness on the one hand, and of swashbuckling and self-righteousness on the other. People with these attitudes do not make good partners in cooperative activity.

We've reduced that situation to manageable proportions in remarkably short time. There are still a few glaring examples of labor leaders whose public pronouncements and actions indicate a desire to play God or the Devil, and an apparent belief they can do so with impunity. There are still some stalwart management defenders of themselves and of most everybody in general against the powers of unions who think of these powers in personal terms, and consequently focus their attack upon individual labor leaders whom they picture as riding high, wide, and handsome over the interests of workers, management, consumers, the bill of rights, mother, home, the flag, and the republican form of government. Such labor leaders make good newspaper copy. They are made to order for dramatic congressional investigations. They provide anti-union pamphleteers with vivid action pictures of unethical, and power-hungry labor bosses whose characteristics, by clever rhetorical manipulation, can be ascribed to other labor leaders for which no adequate evidence of this sort is available.

But today the basic pattern of personal leadership among the new labor men of power, with very few exceptions, is one, not of swashbuckling across the stage in a novel and unaccustomed role, but one of sober and responsible and hard-working acceptance of a tough job, the job of managing an adequate institutional safeguard and expression of the legitimate human interests of 18 million workers and their families in dealings with the management employing these people who constitute the best collection of business and industrial brains, and who manage the largest financial and technical resources, the world has ever known.

There are still some managers who take it as a personal affront that working men and women for whom they, the men of incentive, vision, risk-taking will, and organizing skill, have created and offered jobs, should imagine themselves capable of telling "their superiors" how to run the business. There are still some labor leaders who consider that their chief task is to teach such personal embodiments of class consciousness a lesson. But the basic pattern of reaction among management people to collective bargaining and even to the kind of labor leaders just mentioned, is one not of licking personal wounds of injured vanity, but sober and responsible and hard-working acceptance of a tough job, the job of managing a company so it can get its basic purpose accomplished of producing goods and services at a profit, and doing that in the face of the necessity of sharing essential decisions with the largest number of smart and competent union bargainers this country has ever known.

That's good. Both management and labor leaders on the whole are taking a loss or gain of power less personally, and are more concerned about the impact of the shifting power relations on their companies and unions as *organizations.* Nevertheless the relations between those organizations themselves, and therefore the people who manage them, seem to me to be hardening into a pattern of fairly antagonistic foreign relations between two separate institutions who disagree on many basic issues and in which the chief aim is *dealing* with each other rather than *cooperating* with each other.

Perhaps that is as it must be. I am inclined to think it is. Perhaps it is even as it *should be.* I make no moral judgment about the situation or upon those whose actions in the area of labor and management relations produce that pattern. And before I have finished, I shall hope to make clear that not only are the antagonisms inevitable and legitimate in the relationship, but that their clear and powerful straight-forward expression can lead to productive results if—and it is a big IF—those antagonisms do not harden around the people who hold them so that they lose their capacity to adjust themselves, of course to each other, but equally important, to the changing economic and social conditions that face them with a common challenge. Antagonisms are useful as challenges—not as straightjackets.

Let me restate the basic antagonistic pattern of behavior between the parties which 20 years ago seemed to me to stand in the way of productive relations. Both management and labor leaders appeared to the other to be trying to accumulate or regain power and sovereignty for their own organizations in ways that threatened the power and the sovereignty of the other. My impression is that the dominant pattern of struggling for separate power over the other party and of countering the efforts of the other party is beginning to harden, and that is leading to a hardening of antagonostic predispositions on both sides that makes adjustment more difficult.

That hardening *was* not and *is* not inevitable. It is caused. It is caused 1) by the particular approach the parties have chosen to building up their power. It is caused 2) by frustrations in the effort to develop power internally and with respect to each other. It is caused 3) by emphasis on certain conceptions the parties have about what power is. It is caused 4) by certain methods they have used to accumulate it. It is caused 5) by the concentration of their joint efforts on negative, almost to the exclusion of positive, objectives. It is caused 6) by the failure to conceive of new objectives for partisan effort in the light of the widening scope of issues subjected to joint decision making. These are the things I'd like to talk about here.

The Approach to Power Building

Consider first the approaches organizations might use to build-up their power. I'm going to define the degree of power very simply as the degree of freedom and ability of an organization to accomplish its objectives. What approaches are available for raising that degree?

The first major approach to power accumulation is to improve the organization's own independent internal resources and to use them more effectively and efficiently. That method of developing internal, independent integration, strength, and competent administration may present the other fellow with problems, but such problems are expected and considered a part of the game. They do not *necessarily* lead to antagonism if they are solved by ways which are self-initiated. It is when one party suggests or promotes or makes necessary changes in the internal sources of strength of the other that the resentments mount which increase antagonism. Not many union leaders will deny that just, democratic, and ethical relations between themselves and the rank and file can have, and normally will have, a favorable effect on the development of group solidarity which is the union's basic source of power; but not when the rules designed to promote such relations are imposed upon them by a management backed Landrum-Griffin Act. Many managers would consider some at least of the securities and benefits demanded for workers by unions as advantageous to the development of that organizational power and efficiency rooted in satisfied and loyal work force—if they were introduced on the managers initiative.

Yet this approach to power accumulation through the development of internal organizational strength, even when the pressure comes from the other party, is, in and of itself, unlikely to provide a permanent stimulus to antagonism. The ultimate reward to the party whose internal strength is increased can be counted on to reduce any original resentment at the "arrogance" of the other party.

A second approach is for Organization A to try to influence the decisions and actions of Organization B so that they are compatible with A achieving its purpose. This type of power development is not particularly welcomed by Organization B which is, of course, on the receiving end, but it is recognized as legitimate as long as it does not involve something called "taking unfair advantages." But an unfair advantage is frequently defined as anything A does that exerts enough pressure so that B is not able to choose his course solely on the grounds of advantages to his own organization, or which jockeys B into a position where his choice is really Hobson's choice. There is a tendency for each new strategy and tactic tried by A in order to stimulate B to make his actions and decisions more favorable to the objectives of A, to be challenged by B as unfair. But over time B is likely to develop responsive measures which make less appropriate the characterization of A's strategy and tactics as, by comparison, "unfair." Even the use of force, as in the strike or the lockout or the threat of closing the plant which often puts one party "over the barrel," come in time to be accepted as legitimate when both parties suffer an economic disadvantage, though to varying degrees, and when the action to avoid that disadvantage lies fully within the power of the negotiators. Antagonisms are increased when either party seeks and obtains the assistance of government to limit the other's discretion as to choice of tactics or strategies. This element in the antagonism creating features of industrial relations we shall discuss more fully in a moment.

In any case, however, this approach to the accumulation and use of power, i.e. a reciprocal effort to influence the actions and decisions of each other, is the very essence of collective bargaining. Indeed it is an essential element in industrial relations even, and in a sense particularly, in the absence of collective bargaining. Collective bargaining, however far short of the mark it may to date have fallen, has grown up as a social device for reducing the injustices and frustrations and lack of control of the individual over his degree of security and progress in the employment relationship when that relationship is ultimately controlled unilaterally by the employer. These injustices and frustrations and lack of control are the real generators of antagonisms among employees, antagonisms which in the absence of the opportunity to participate in the determination and administration of the terms of employment can harden into class antagonisms. The reduction of such class antagonisms is a more nearly impossible task than the reduction of those which grow up in the experience of collective bargaining between unions and management. In the latter case there is at least the possibility of *mutual effort* to arrive at a consensus on terms of employment providing *mutual benefits* for employers, unions, and the workers they represent, and a *mutual commitment* to *mutual survival.*

The third avenue to the acquisition of power is the one that really makes the parties angry. It is the method of weakening one's competitor, or limiting the things he is permitted to do. Specific reference to strategy and tactics characteristic of this approach will be made in the discussion of other causes of hardening of antagonisms which follow.

There is still another way Organization A can achieve power, or the freedom and ability to reach its objectives, whenever the reaching involves joint effort with Organization B. That is to contribute to increasing the resources and active strength of Organization B so that B's collaboration can be more effective in that associated activity for the achieving of goals important to both of them. It may appear to some of you who read these words that even to mention this last possibility is evidence that I am an unregenerated Utopian. The truth is that I am. But that shall not prevent me from acknowledging that this last form of power accumulation has aroused relatively little enthusiasm, and even less energetic effort, from the parties involved in the last twenty years.

Here we have at least four avenues to power accumulation. All have been used during the past two decades. But each party gets the impression that the other is working especially hard on the second and third approaches. That is, they see the other organization trying to increase its own power by acting on them, especially by using methods which are considered coercive and therefore unfair, or by attempting to weaken them or limit the activities permitted them. Their reaction to such attempts is short and bitter: "They are trying to cut us down to size." That general conclusion sets the tone of the relationship and colors the interpretation placed upon many relatively insignificant actions.

Frustrations from Arrested Growth

A *second* factor which increases the tendency toward a hardening of antagonisms is related to frustrations attendant upon the slowing down of the rate of growth in union membership. The peak of around 17½ million was reached in 1956. By 1961 the total was down to around 16½ million, and the latest figures (1965) available at this time indicate a membership of less than 17 million. In view of the fact that the civilian labor force is constantly increasing, the *percentage* of workers organized was of course actually decreasing from about 25% in 1956 to about 22% in 1965. In the last 14 years the percentage of N.L.R.B. elections won and of votes cast for unions has declined from the low seventies to the low sixties.

This arresting of union growth has caused much soul-searching among union leaders, although not all would agree with one of their ablest spokesmen that the situation constitutes a "crisis." Nor are they inclined to put the whole blame on a toughened approach of management to resisting union organization, particularly in the South and among white collar workers where the large increases in the labor force are taking place. They are willing to admit that the increasingly numerically significant white collar workers particularly in the services and in government occupations are not attracted by the traditional organizing tactics and promises developed for organizing blue collar production workers, and that they have not adapted their message to make it persuasively attractive. They are aware that they have cultivated successfully the organization of workers in large enterprises in the most heavily industrialized sections of the country and that the remaining task of "mopping up" in smaller companies and semi-rural districts is comparatively more difficult. Some of them are inclined to assess their very past successes in winning benefits, not only for union members but indirectly for all workers, as a cause of the decline in interest of the unorganized to sign up. As one of them remarked, "Maybe we have benefited ourselves out of the market." They recognize in very straightforward debate among themselves that much fault lies in their own failure to develop up to date structure and methods to meet changing organizing problems in changing industrial circumstances, and that they have not solved the problem of jurisdictional rivalries which weaken their efforts. Yet the increasing effectiveness and sophistication of managements in their efforts to limit or prevent the organization of their employees looms larger as a stimulus to antagonistic reactions in a situation of arrested growth than it would in a situation of expanding membership in spite of such management efforts. Management who under the latter situation would simply be labeled as "tough competitors" now are labeled as "19th Century reactionaries," "unregenerated profiteers," "descendants of the robber barons," etc. The names are important chiefly because they reveal a perpetuation or revival of the antagonisms characterizing an earlier period of industrial relations.

Concepts about Power

Third, the parties have contributed to a hardening of the antagonistic elements in their relationship by the action content they have given to the concept of power. I'm not concerned at the moment whether these operational definitions are right or wrong. But right or wrong, defensible or not, they are the meanings which one party uses to appraise its own and the other party's actions, and decide what they ought to do about it. And what they are doing about it seems to me to be resulting in a hardening of the relationship into what Summer called "antagonistic cooperation," but with the emphasis on the first word. What are some of these working conceptions of power?

In the first place management and labor leaders have been chiefly concerned with power as *relative* power. Make no mistake, they *have to be* concerned with the relative aspects of power. But when that idea *predominates,* the leaders of each organization look at the successful or unsuccessful efforts of the other to develop even *internal* strength, as something which decreases or increases respectively the strength of their own organization. When power is considered to be almost exclusively relative power, it is a common sense inference that if the other party gets stronger, you get weaker, and if he has less power, you have more.

Now it is no secret that most companies and unions in the United States have grown considerably in their power to bargain. Internally they are getting stronger, better organized, more skillful in bargaining, better prepared to bargain, more sophisticated, and better able to take a strike if bargaining breaks down. Both management and union leaders know that about the other because the job of bargaining gets tougher each time. This is an experience every leader on both sides has. Now if he is almost exclusively preoccupied with the idea that power is *relative* power, the experience creates an anxiety about his ability to keep his organization up in the race. The other party he feels is getting *too* strong. This basic anxiety, I want to emphasize, is created by an immediate and vivid experience every one has. It is not created, it is only embellished and given support, by the polemics against big labor monopolies on the one hand and big business oligarchies on the other. But against the background of that personal experience that the other party is getting harder, not easier, to deal with, it is easy to accept the polemics as gospel. And according to that gospel, when one party gets stronger, the other becomes relatively weaker.

One way in which internal independent power of a company or union can be developed is by getting employees or members to be more enthusiastic and active and cooperative in the interests of the company or union, as the case may be. Any manager or leader of any organization has to do that. It is just one of his elementary jobs. Whether one calls it developing good team work and workmanship, as management does, or group solidarity, as the union leaders do, one is talking about what everyone knows is an important organizational power resource and is essential if the organization is to function at all. Moreover, I can't imagine any more difficult job over the long pull for either management or labor leaders than having to bargain with an organization whose members or employees aren't genuinely committed to the welfare of their union or their company respectively.

One might think, therefore, that each party would welcome, or at least not be worried about, the best possible job the other is doing in developing this kind of internal power. Not when folks are preoccupied with the relative aspects of power. When that is the point of view that dominates, this legitimate process of internal integration is looked at as a *competition* for loyalty, and every evidence of success of one leadership is looked upon by the other as a defeat of its own efforts.

In spite of conclusions, well documented by research, that this loyalty issue is a false one in most circumstances and that dual loyalties are not only possible but natural, this antagonism-generating interpretation of the efforts of leaders to integrate participants around their own organizational objectives still persists.

It persists in the minds of labor leaders as well as of management. Note the recurrent allegations of labor leaders that management's human relations efforts are just another way of trying to transfer the loyalties of workers from the union to the company.

Note the apparent verification of this suspicion by the efforts of some managements to preserve the development and administration of benefits and various types of bonuses as an area of unilateral company action, and their concern about forestalling union organization among occupational groups not yet organized by setting up human relations programs for them. Note further the allegations by management leaders that the union leaders in attempting to develop group solidarity among their members consider the strike an excellent way to do this, and, further that to hear them talk, all the improvements in the conditions of life for workers have been wrung from an unwilling foot-dragging, and inhuman management by their union.

I don't cite these examples to criticize what leaders are doing to make workers enthusiastic and loyal supporters of the company or the union, nor to criticize their reaction to what the other fellow is doing. That reaction is natural when one thinks of the power one is trying to develop, through participant support, as *relative* power. But that reaction is one of the factors hardening the relationship of antagonistic cooperation in the direction of antagonism rather than cooperation.

Let me repeat. The concern with relative power is legitimate and absolutely necessary in any situation where two organizations are trying, as they are in industrial relations, to influence the actions of each other. I'm talking about what happens when that is the *only* kind of power they can think of. That leads them to interpret the increase in internal power of the other as something taken away from them, and that interpretation hardens antagonisms.

Another idea about power which has a bearing on the hardening of antagonisms is the very natural one that power is a function of being able to use tried and tested methods. It follows that management and union leaders believe they are *losing* power when they have to change their methods of operation, when conditions make it necessary for them to place less reliance on the traditional methods they are trained in and used to. They have got used to thinking of those methods not only as right, but the freedom to use them as their right. Finding it difficult or impossible to use them, they feel they have lost power.

The situation I'm referring to is well known to every manager and union leader. The entrance of the union was the condition that faced management with this necessity. It is not an exaggeration to say that when collective bargaining became a part of operations of a company, managerial methods underwent a revolution greater than would have been the case if those companies had been nationalized. That revolution, to define it very briefly but adeqately, was this. Company managers became virtually *co-managers* with labor leaders in limited but expanding areas where they were formerly *solo* managers, in setting a whole set of high level and general company policies in those areas and in the detailed execution of those policies. And the labor leader "co-manager" was not accountable to the same higher authority who held the company manager responsible for the results of his decisions and acts. Anyone who thinks that the shift from a single line managership to this type of virtual co-managership didn't involve a revolution in the methods of organizational decision making and operations is either blind or uninformed.

It is no wonder that company managers interpreted this necessity to change old methods and take up and learn new ones as a loss in power. The loss of power to get things done *in the old familiar ways,* under the old arrangements of authority and accountability, is understandably interpreted as the loss of power—*period.* Today the early reaction in the face of this revolution—"protect and maintain managerial *prerogatives,*" has been rephrased. The present position is "preserve necessary managerial *functions* for agents of the company." The change is merely literary. The issue is the same. And it will take more than one generation of managers to work out the orientation and methods appropriate to the situation. And they cannot work it out alone. The union leaders will see to that.

The President's Conference right after the war broke up essentially because of the inability to resolve that issue. If another such conference held today didn't suffer the same fate, it would be because the parties agreed to avoid the issue. To the credit of American managers in general, let it be said that on the whole they've stopped *talking* general principles on this matter and are *acting* on each case as it arises. But the underlying strategy and mood is that of a rear-guard action seeking to restrict the union's encroachment on their freedom and discretion in managing. And every time a new regulation of that freedom gets into a contract, or follows from a N.L.R.B. decision on "failure to bargain in good faith" relative to an unfair labor practice brought by a union, management feels it has lost just that much power. Their perception of the situation is that the union which demanded and got the regulation has succeeded in their effort to cut management's power down to size. And I don't think any union man will deny that that *is* the objective.

The unions also face attempts to restrict their use of traditional methods. They also look at the failure successfully to resist these attempts as a loss of power. But the changing situation has called into question old methods for them as it has for management. The traditional methods of unions were born in an era of desperate struggle even for recognition and the right to exist at all. The last stages of that struggle before the rapid growth of unions in the Thirties and the Forties was a knock-down and drag-out civil war. Moreover, outside of a few unions like those on the railroads and in coal, the area of effective bargaining was relatively restricted and the damage caused by disputes and struggles didn't run like blood poisoning through the arteries of the whole economy. In that atmosphere developed methods of reasonable and peaceful negotiation and bargaining wherever these were possible. But there were developed as well the tactics to be used when negotiations broke down or were refused. And since they had to count on these methods so often, their effective use was equated with union power: the organizational strike, the strike to force specific demands, the sympathy strike, the demonstration strike, mass picketing, the boycott both primary and secondary, on-the-job action including the slowdown and sabotage, and some of the less savory kinds of racketeering and coercive tactics directed both against the slow joiners and anti-union employers. Even the trade agreement was in many cases a treaty of temporary peace setting forth the terms imposed by the victor on the vanquished.

To the credit of this generation of labor leaders, let it be said that they are aware as anyone that they occupy a critical place in American society, and make decisions which greatly affect the public interest, and that their methods will have to be appropriate to that kind of a responsibility. And they know that this situation, as much as the management stimulated public police power, is forcing them to revise old, and devise new, methods. They know that their growth in size and influence, the legal status they now enjoy, the provision of public instruments like the representation election and the unfair labor practice procedure, the necessity for winning public approval, have made it necessary and desirable for them to take a cold and critical look at some of these methods. In the light of their newness to the job, they have depended to a surprising degree on the instruments of peaceful organization and negotiation.

But, as in the case of management, it would be surprising if they didn't fight to prevent any curtailment of their right to use traditional methods and access such curtailment as a loss of power. Unions have their own version of managerial-prerogative action. They resist modification of what they claim as a right to picket, to strike, to boycott, to enforce the use of union made materials, and to compel union membership by union shop arrangements in place of the old-fashioned methods either of evangelical persuasion or coercive pressure.

And when they see the management people they deal with supporting legislation to restrict them in these methods which union leaders look on as "union prerogatives," it is at least understandable that they consider this to be evidence that management would like to cut them down to size. And I don't think any management man would deny that that *is* their objective.

Both union and management leaders reflect the mood of Colonel Blimp, Mr. Lowe's cartoon character representing the average John Bullish Englishman, who reacted to the postwar "breaking up" of the power and possessions of the British Empire in these words, "I'm against it. As for me, I'm for holding on to all we've got—if we can get it back."

I still believe that in time management will see that the path to their power lies in developing the methods and skills appropriate to the virtual situation of *co-managership* that they face. I still believe that in time union leaders will see that their path to power lies in developing the methods and skills appropriate to the virtual situation of *co-responsibility* they face for keeping a delicate and complicated job- and product-providing industry in efficient operation. I still believe that when that day arrives, both will wonder why they interpreted the necessity to develop *new* methods for gaining and using power as a *loss* of power. But in the meantime that interpretation and the suspicion that the other party, in attempting to restrict their reliance on traditional methods, is trying to cut them down to size emphasizes the word "antagonistic" in the pattern of antagonistic cooperation which now describes their relationships.

Identification of Corruption, Size and Power

Two more ways of thinking about power have contributed to an increase in antagonistic elements in union-management relations. The first is the identification of size with power, the second is the confusion of corruption and power.

Management people are not necessarily the ones who created the confusion with respect to unions. But enough of them have joined in the discussion to give union leaders the impression that they unconsciously or intentionally contribute to such ideas and are ready to use them at the drop of a hat, if to do so would reduce the effectiveness of the pressures unions are now able to bring on management.

Union leaders are not the only ones who have created the confusion with respect to companies. But they have a long tradition dating back into the 19th Century of using such allegations with respect to the managements who resist, (particularly those who resist successfully), the organization of their employees, and who are powerful enough to deal at arms length with unions even when the unions have been recognized as the representatives of those employees.

The continued pronouncements and lobbying of prominent employers and employers associations to get the antitrust laws applied to unions, to prevent unions from organizing and representing the employees of more than one employer, to prohibit them from carrying on collective bargaining for the employees of competing employers, to restrict industry-wide bargaining, and their reference to the union of the A.F.L. and the C.I.O. in 1955 as the formation of a giant monoply have put labor union leaders on notice that some influential managements are ready to challenge union power by literally "cutting them down to size."

The union leaders have no legislative program or private strategies for reducing the size of the employer units they deal with, but their careless reference to employers in general as if they had the power characteristics of the mammoth units included in the 200 largest corporations is a source of antagonistic resentment on the part of hundreds of thousands of employers who run companies of relatively small size.

The identification of power and corruption is an even greater source of hardening antagonisms. Particularly when such identification, appropriately characterizing *some* companies and *some* unions, is used to discredit a particular employer or a particular union involved in an organizing campaign, is this considered a "low blow." Both union leaders and management are now permitted a large degree of "free speech" in promoting enthusiasm for or against unions in organizing campaigns. Employers who, in the effort to turn their employees against a particular union, characterize all unions in terms of the unethical practices and skulduggery to be found in some of them, make a great contribution to the hardening of antagonisms. The union leaders who engage in this sort of antagonism producing free speech are not as fortunate as those employers who care to do so in having at their disposal the 40 volumes of testimony from the McClellan Committee investigations of corrupt practices and lack of democratic procedures in unions, but the record of off-color company practices provides them with enough ammunition for their purpose.

There are obvious relations between power and corruption and between power and size. They are too complicated to discuss here. My point is that the simple grouping of these concepts as practically identical with each other and the use of evidence of one to infer the existence of the others has kept the discussion of such matters on a pretty low level where antagonistic emotions have a good chance to germinate.

Ways of Implementing Power

Now let us turn from the way the parties think about power to the methods they've used to increase their power. It is taken for granted that any use of force or violence will contribute to the hardening of antagonisms between management and labor leaders. It is unlikely that the negotiating of collective bargaining agreements will ever be carried out in private industry, in all instances, without the threat or the use of this demonstration of ultimate power. It is too clear that the freedom *to* contract is an empty phrase without freedom *not to* contract when the parties who are the chief sufferers from such an interruption of productive work are also the chief interested parties whose advantage or disadvantage is to be served by the outcome of their negotiations.

Yet it is encouraging to note that the use of the strike, and the antagonisms it generates between the parties, is less now than when *Mutual Survival* was written. Indeed it might be asserted that, with time lost from strikes accounting for less than two-tenths of one percent of total working time, we have almost reached the irreducible minimum. From the point of view of the factors contributing to the increase or reduction of antagonisms between management, unions, and workers, this reduction in time lost through strikes is a reduction in time spent in an experience which not only generates antagonisms, but is, like war, an operation which requires that antagonisms be strengthened and even created.

The most notable development over the twenty years, however, is that strikes over organization and recognition disputes have largely been replaced by the use of the N.L.R.B. election procedures. This was a type of strike which really aroused antagonism colored by bitterness.

It is clear that there is a growing tendency for the public to focus its ire on those unions engaging in strikes in essential industries and services where a major casualty is the public's interest. At this point, however, our interest is in the hardening or easing of antagonisms between management and unions and workers. From the point of view of that interest the decreasing resort to the strike weapon is a major source of encouragement.

But two other methods increasingly used during these 20 years have had a different result. I refer to certain kinds of political and legal action and to the extension of alliances.

Political and legal action has this effect largely because it throws issues into an arena where they have to be simply and dogmatically stated in terms that will get a desired response from people who really don't know what the issues are all about. And I'm talking now not just about citizens in an election or referendum, but about the majority of legislators, and even some of the judges and servants of administrative agencies. If one wants to influence people in that kind of a situation, partisan positions have to be taken and held firmly, and once and for all. Also they are likely to be linked up with high sounding principles so that unwillingness to desert those principles becomes a matter of honor. Once the issue is laid down in the political arena there is little to do but fight on to victory or defeat. You don't change your platform in the middle of a campaign nor your case before administrative agency or court before the judgment is given.

I expressed a faith in 1946, which I now reaffirm, that the power relations on the *collective bargaining front* will eventually move away from their present hardening antagonistic pattern. One of the reasons for that faith is that the dealings between parties at the bargaining table are immediate and direct, and the ideas and methods used are subject to immediate testing and correction.

But the antagonistic relations developed between opponents in the attempt to obtain legal immunities and impose legal restrictions of a general sort don't have the same chance to get resolved by the give and take of face-to-face negotiation and other kinds of practical dealings with one another.

Notice I'm not talking about *all* kinds of political and government agency action. I'm talking about efforts to gain advantages in collective bargaining through obtaining the partisan assistance of government. Even that kind, of course, may be necessary. If so, we must accept the consequences. To the degree that the struggle for increasing one's own power position and cutting the other's power position down to size takes place in the area of legislative, administrative agency, and court determinations instead of in the area of collective bargaining, we may expect a continued hardening of the antagonisms. Don't misunderstand this as a case against political action. I'm just pointing out cause and effect. I give you just one example. Is there any doubt that the campaign for and against right-to-work laws has created more lasting hardened antagonisms than the whole series of attempts to get the union shop or to avoid it through collective bargaining?

Another method which is natural and inevitable, but which has contributed to this result is the way both parties have widened their alliances in order to gain advantages in dealing with each other. This does not necessarily mean that formal multiple-company bargaining has shown any marked increase except perhaps on the West Coast. But the lending of formal and informal strike aid, the informal agreements to stick together, the mapping of common strategy and policy in negotiations does seem to be on the increase. It has, of course, long been a union approach to increase unit power by making alliances for mutual aid and support and action. Now management appears to be stepping up such an approach, for instance, in air transport, trucking, shipping, newspapers, and possibly in autos and steel. Notice that alliances are normally intended to support a party in antagonistic relations.

The broadening out of alliances leads to the hardening of whatever pattern of relationship exists if for no other reason than that the larger the number of units involved, the greater the need to stabilize the kinds of strategies and tactics to be used and the philosophies that legitimize the actions. People and organizations engaged in joint supportive action must know what to expect from each other, and that makes adjustment in methods and principles and even in their shared emotions less likely.

Concentration on Conflict Areas

Another factor which has tended to harden some of the antagonistic elements in the relationship between management and labor is one which will be with us to the end. The contacts which leaders in both groups have with each other tend inevitably to focus on points of disagreement between them. And those disagreements are honest and deep-seated ones over objectives, and ideas of how to reach them, held by people who manage and people who are managed, held by people who have to meet a payroll and those whose livelihood depends on being on that payroll. Such disagreements can be reduced or compromised but not removed. To be sure, the whole process of negotiating the trade agreement and the whole process of grievance settlement is an attempt to reduce disagreements. But that doesn't change the fact that the subject matter dealt with in the relationship *is* normally a disagreement. That's no one's fault. It's one basic reason we have collective bargaining. But negative and antagonistic reactions and feelings are likely to be sharpened up with practice in that kind of a situation.

Twenty years ago I thought I saw a tendency for union leaders and managements in some quarters to tackle together problems on which there was no necessary disagreement between them. I thought this might reduce some of the antagonism built up in fighting over necessary and legitimate disagreements. There are examples of this, but not enough to set the general tone of the relationship. It is possible to report, however, that responsible spokesmen on both sides are asking such questions as the following:

"Is there any inevitable reason why there should be a conflict between a management and a union position on such matters as: cost and waste reduction, safety promotion, technological improvement, automation, training programs, the improvement of standards and administration of unemployment insurance, workmen's compensation, health insurance?" "Is there any reason why joint discussions shouldn't be undertaken to clarify objectives, analyze facts, and even why common action shouldn't be taken with respect to *such* matters as well as with respect to such larger issues as maintenance of full employment, control of inflationary forces, rehabilitation of depressed areas?"

I am aware that there are objections on both sides to joint activity on many such issues, particularly those involved in planning for and operating plants. Handling some of them would require, for instance, a sharing with union people of figures which most managers think can't be disclosed that way. Many managers object that any such move would be an abdication of functions that should be exclusively their responsibility. Union leaders in many cases are also careful about getting involved in joint action, the results of which they might wish later to challenge as disadvantageous to their members. They don't want to be charged with playing footsie with management. Anyone familiar with developments over the past 20 years knows how many times some such moves have been suggested from both sides, and how frequently they have foundered on just such craggy rocks as these.

But this serves only to point up the situation I'm discussing here. Parties whose relations are chiefly over disagreements find their antagonisms as well as their cooperative tendencies fed by their contacts. And because that has been the kind of contacts most management and labor leaders have had with each other, their antagonistic predispositions have had at least as much practice as, and probably more practice than, their cooperative predispositions.

The Need for New Strategies

A final factor contributes not so much to the hardening of antagonisms as to the loss of opportunity to reduce them. That factor stems from the predisposition of both parties to adhere frequently to a philosophy, strategy, and tactics that are adapted more to the problems of the past than to the possibilities of the future. They chart their course more from memory than from vision. The power of both management and union leaders today and tomorrow will have to lie in their ability to launch a program that meets the challenge set up for them by today's and tomorrow's industry, economy, and society, and by the unfinished business of making democracy a reality in the world of work. Whatever some of their thoughtful and future-oriented leaders say, the actions of many unions and companies speak louder than words, and those actions show more grasp of what was needed in the past than of what the future demands. Nothing can prevent a union, or a company, or an army, or a college, or a church, or a nation from losing the power to do its future job, if their philosophy and strategy and tactics don't fit that job. They'll end up as the March Hare did when he tried to fix the Mad Hatter's watch with butter. In the face of inevitable failure, all he could say was "And it was the best butter, too. The best butter."

It's clear that the old battlecry of the unions "We'll *get* more, and more, and more *now*" is less appropriate today as a *summation* of purposes than it was at a time when workers were starving while companies accumulated the fat that might reduce their hunger. What is called for is something that sounds more like "We'll join to *produce* more and more, now and in the future." The emphasis on building walls around particular jobs and making them the property of particular people, and the whole set of security practices summed up in the terms "featherbedding" and "seniority rights" were of course adjustments to the terrible insecurities for individual workers yesterday. They always will have a place—but one which is secondary—and very much secondary today and tomorrow—to the emphasis on increasing the productivity and long range profitability of industries which are increasingly under severe competition from industrially aroused and productively growing nations of the world. There's no security for anyone unless that emphasis is made and made to work. The shortsightedness of preoccupation with the unions in protecting their jurisdiction over specific job territories when automation is rapidly wiping out the jobs they seek jurisdiction over should be self-evident. The emphasis on the shorter work week as the primary cure for the problems raised by structural unemployment while at the same time stressing the great unsatisfied needs of the workers of the country for more goods and services reveals, to say the least, a narrow analysis of what is required in order to achieve both of these objectives.

Let me say at once that no one of these emphases in union strategy and technique can be abandoned as a *part* of their program. The threat to the unions' power is not that these things are in their program, but that they are *primary* things. They are traditional approaches that were hammered out and which worked successfully in the attempt to lift several generations of workers from industrial serfdom to a self-respecting position in American society and to gain for them the means and collective strength to maintain and exercise the rights and duties of that position. And there are places in American society where that is still necessary.

When it comes to the kind of program geared not so much to protecting workers against exploitation and unions from extinction, but rather to releasing and putting to work the potential of workers, unions, *and* management, and an automated industry, and a free Democratic political system for security, survival and progress, however, the union leaders' program can't depend on what they themselves plan and do. It will have to be planned and done in collaboration with management. Union philosophy and strategy and the ways to implement both are going to have to involve joint decisions and actions with management. That will be clear when we look for evidence that union leaders and management *are* taking the first faltering steps in this direction.

Frankly I don't see any large scale new and challenging vision among management people which gives them guide lines for harnessing and integrating the potential in workers, union leaders, automated industry and a free political system for the security, survival and progress of all of us in this country. Their guide lines for the future are also those that worked successfully for them and for the economy in the past. What is their expressed solution? It is this: "Carry on. Increase the effectiveness of our technology and capital investment to produce more with less manpower. Free us managers from the restrictions of unions and government to run our business as we think best without interference. Compensate people who get hurt through unemployment, accident, early obsolescence, with as much as we have to, in order to meet their demands and keep them working for us as long as we need them. And promise a long range security to their children." There is nothing new in that program.

Notice this about the approach of both unions and management. Neither of them puts their faith in releasing the creative and productive abilities of and giving expression to those abilities in the great body of working people. The unions are striving to make these people secure by protecting them against the controls exercised over their lives by management. They are depending on regulating management, and in the process they are hamstringing management in its attempts to use its brains and skills for more effective production. But at the same time they are channeling the workers brains and skill toward practices that limit production instead of pointing the way toward and releasing their energies for greater effort and contributions to increasing it. This is the case even though their sincere purpose is to increase the individual member's security in his job and income in the light of their suspicion that management left to its own unilateral discretion would handle things in a way that would decrease the individuals security and income. They are putting their emphasis on regulating management and in the process they necessarily regulate the workers as well.

Management if they have any concern for the general economy and for the people who work for them, are counting on machines and money and their managerial freedom to make these people or their children more secure in the future than they are now. Without for a moment underestimating the tremendous possibilities in this triumvirate of resources, i.e. machines, money, and management, the consequence of sole reliance on them is that any contributions from any other source, union leaders, workers, foremen, and even many in junior management, are discouraged and the potential in them lies untapped.

With a few exceptions, neither is concerned about setting up arrangements that will tap for the benefit of industry, productivity, and profitability, and ultimately for the nation the unused capacities and skills and inventiveness and voluntary energy of the 70 million folks who work for and are paid wages for working for somebody else.

I can't see any *general* rush on the part of either union leaders or management to activate industrial relations programs along these lines, but there are some hope-providing experiments, which, if they were to spread more widely, might counteract some of the tendencies we have noted toward a hardening of antagonisms.

Some of these experiments have to do with planning for and protecting the interests of all concerned in the process of automation. In these plans there has been union and worker agreement to reduce the outmoded insistence on rigid occupational boundaries and restrictions on productive output in exchange for funds and arrangements to provide retraining, transfer, and compensation for those who get hurt in the process and to study the whole program of change over and plan for carrying it out. And the workers representatives, that is the unions, are participating in that study and planning. These experiments are being carried on at Armour, and on the West Coast docks, interestingly enough, by Harry Bridges' union (I.L.W.U.) and the Pacific Maritime Association.

Another plan tried out chiefly in smaller firms is one in which joint union and management departmental and plant committees figure out together each month how to reduce the size of the direct labor cost in relation to some other variable, like total sales, and distribute as a bonus any saving made. Here also the progressive feature is the participation of the union in analyzing and planning, and in the development of worker interest in and responsibility for, and pressure on, their fellow workers for increasing, not limiting, production. These experiments are known as the Scanlon Plan.

A third type of experiment is the joint negotiation and administration of a profit-, or rather progress-sharing system such as was recently worked out in American Motors and Kaiser. There are other examples of profit-sharing worked out and administered jointly by unions and management in smaller companies, although for the most part they have been planned and administered unilaterally without consultation with the unions and frequently as a device to keep the union from getting a hold in the plant.

Another type of experiment which appears to have promise and is being tried in an increasing number of places is what might be called the "continuous negotiation," though "continuous study, analysis, and problem solving" fits the practice better. It is typified both by the Steel Human Relations Committee and by the Kaiser plan mentioned above. Unpressured by the time restraints and emotional intensities of the periodic concentrated bargaining sessions, management and union leaders (and, in the Kaiser plan, public members also) engage in ongoing explorations of the nature of emerging problems and seek for ways of meeting them.

No one can say how these experiments will fare in the long run, but they have certain features that are forward looking and could encourage unions *and* management to adopt the philosophy and strategy of increasing efforts toward greater productivity instead of limiting it, and in the process learn the ways favorable not only to mutual survival but to mutual benefit.

One feature is the recognition that everyone in the enterprise, including the workers, have contributions of mind and skill to make in analyzing problems and planning for their solution and motivating performance.

Another feature is the recognition that there are real and stubborn fears of being displaced by machines that are based in bitter experience, and that, until these are reduced, the traditional protective devices of restricting production and managerial discretion in technological and managerial innovation will be used to back up union efforts to regulate management initiative in this area.

Another feature in some plans is that an attempt is made to reduce this fear by setting aside a major fund, which might be called a human-depreciation reserve, as evidence not only that management is serious about avoiding the human costs, but will have the funds available to back up their good intentions.

A very significant feature, of the progress or profit sharing schemes in particular, is that the workers have a chance to feel they are working for themselves in building up a stake in the future profitability of the company. They are working for a share in that profitability and not just for wages paid to human tools used to produce profits.

Another feature is that the term "collective bargaining" as descriptive of an ongoing relationship has been broadened to encompass "collective problem solving."

Most important of all is the chance for workers to participate through their representatives not just in bargaining over the results of their work but in planning and administering the equipment and arrangements for doing that work.

In Conclusion

Twenty years of experience in dealing with each other leaves the basic situation of antagonistic cooperation pretty much unchanged. And unless our experience is different from that of any other industrial nation, I suspect it will continue that way. In itself that is nothing to be worried about. Antagonistic cooperation has characterized a great share of the adjustments between forces both in nature and society.

When two groups of people have to resolve very fundamental differences of objective and method on the operational level, antagonistic cooperation is what should be expected. Whatever *ultimate* common goals may be in terms of a healthy economy, and a healthy, capable, and public spirited citizenry, there are *on the operational level,* real and honest immediate differences and disagreements between the people who work and the people they work for.

I have pointed out some of the circumstances that at the moment have pushed that antagonistic cooperation toward the antagonistic end of the scale. The consequence I regret, however, is not the degree of antagonism, but the *hardening* of those antagonisms in a way that makes adjustive and adaptive cooperation more difficult in the face of a dynamic changing economy that will challenge all the capacity for adjustment and cooperation both management and labor can muster. But cooperation there *has* been and cooperation there *must* be, simply because the companies who employ the workers and the unions who bargain for the workers need each other.

The unions need the cooperation of management. They need all the skill and power management can muster to provide the plans and resources and organization of effort that add up to expanding job opportunities and products, the amount and quality of which necessarily determine the economic and even social status of their members. The unions need management if for no other reason than to have someone to bargain with.

And whether they admit it or not, the management of those companies in which their employees desire collective representation need the cooperation of unions. They need the unions to bring to a focus on their decision-making the needs of and pressures from the workers they employ. It is a mistaken notion that the unions *created* those needs and pressures. They were always there—but in major sectors of industrial operations workers did not find, and do not now find, adequate and effective expression except through the services of a union.

Antagonistic cooperation will continue to swing back and forth between the poles of antagonism and cooperation, but management and union leaders are locked together in a joint enterprise in which neither can do without the other. Too much antagonism is self defeating. A hardening of antagonisms is crippling to adaptive effort. But I would also venture to say that too much cooperation, at least some kinds of cooperation, is self defeating. It is not to the benefit of the members of unions if management cooperates by rolling over and does not do its best to watch its costs, maintain systematic and orderly organization, the right to make necessary decisions, and to allocate the proceeds of production to the continued improvement of the instruments of production, including both men and machines. And it is not to the benefit of management if the union leaders become so much a cooperative arm of management that the unions lose their power to present forcefully and effectively the needs and demands of workers for an increasing standard of living and an increasing voice in making the rules and controlling the conditions under which they work and live.

If each does that job well, he is cooperating with the other party, whether that party gives him credit for it or not. Riding on the maintenance and improvement of that kind of antagonistic cooperation are not only the mutual survival of free unions and free management, but the survival of a free society.